Jericho
& other stories & poems

Rowan B Fortune
(editor)

Published by Cinnamon Press
Meirion House
Glan yr afon
Tanygrisiau
Blaenau Ffestiniog
Gwynedd LL41 3SU
www.cinnamonpress.com

The right of the contributors to be identified as the authors of this work has been asserted by them in accordance with the Copyright, Designs and Patent Act, 1988. © 2012
ISBN 978-1-907090-67-7
British Library Cataloguing in Publication Data. A CIP record for this book can be obtained from the British Library

All rights reserved. No part of this publication may be reproduced, stored in a retrieval system, or transmitted in any form or by any means, electronic, mechanical, photocopying, recording or otherwise without the prior written permission of the publishers. This book may not be lent, hired out, resold or otherwise disposed of by way of trade in any form of binding or cover other than that in which it is published, without the prior consent of the publishers.

Designed and typeset in Palatino and Garamond by Cinnamon Press.
Cover design by Jan Fortune-Wood from original artwork 'Old Locomotive' © Iakov Philimonov, agency dreamtime.

Cinnamon Press is represented by Inpress and by the Welsh Books Council in Wales.

Printed in Poland

Introduction

Short stories and poems are mediums placed to grasp incidents on the margins, life's fragmentary happenings. Joanna Campbell's 'Ten O'clock To Balham' and Vivian Hassan-Lambert's titular 'Jericho' are located on trains; they occupy those tense, waiting, public spaces of intermediary time. And in different ways each throws up a character against historically grounded social milieus and plays the incident off reader expectations. They create the tone for the rest of the book's tales.

In his poem 'Waiver' Edward Ragg gives an ode to the margins of text itself; or texts limits, 'the insistent/ Gift of the unwritten.' The depth of Ragg ideas is belied by the delicacy and the preciseness of his metaphorical language. 'As if the sky was lit/ With the nomenclature/ Of the vivid;' ('The Taking of the Capital'). Ian McEwan deploys repetition in 'The gale blows itself out', which mounts tension and renders something arbitrary and disturbing in a haunting philosophy, 'As you sleep the wind's accidents/ bluster and gust/ hand us through hugeness:/ because nothing./ One bird in the gale.' Both are united in expressing the world in light touches.

Rowan B. Fortune
Tŷ Meirion, June 2012

Contents

Ten O'clock to Balham by Joanna Campbell	9
Urashima by Lindsey Holland	15
Beowulf by Lindsey Holland	16
Sigurd and Fafnir by Lindsey Holland	17
Waiver by Edward Ragg	18
The Entire Scale by Edward Ragg	19
The Taking of the Capital by Edward Ragg	20
Afterwords by Edward Ragg	21
Exhibition by Gemma Green	22
Hertz by Gemma Green	23
Afternoon Telly by Frances Corkey Thompson	24
High by Jacqueline Haskell	25
The Female Snowy Owl by Martin Willitts Jr	33
The Snow Queen by Martin Willitts Jr	34
Here's Madness by Jill Teague	36
War Paint by Jill Teague	37
Looking Over Strange Terrain by David Ford	38
Man and boy in a mirror by David Ford	39
Lily and The Blue Book by Lindsey Stanberry-Flynn	40
The priest offers haircuts by Phil Madden	50
Origami Haiku by Phil Madden	51
The Fox on the Moor by Phil Madden	52
Dreamcatcher by Anna Johnson	53
Crucifix by Anna Johnson	54
Malta by Clare Dyer	55
Dowry (i) by Clare Dyer	56
Dowry (ii) by Clare Dyer	57
The British Museum At 60 *Modigliani* by Margaret Wilmot	58
Caryatid, *Modigliani* by Margaret Wilmot	60
Bewildered by Anthony Howcroft	61
The Night Worker by Jane McLaughlin	67
How to Make a Cloud by Jane McLaughlin	68
Tea by Jane McLaughlin	69
The Ending Was In the Beginning by Richard Williams	70
Plumage by David Olsen	71
Summer Rain by David Olsen	72
A Cup of Tea by Patricia Helen Wooldridge	73
In The Museum by Patricia Helen Wooldridge	74
Set in Amber by Lezanne Clannachan	75

Erosion by Rosalind Hudis	83
Heart Patch by Rosalind Hudis	84
Platinum by Maria Grech Ganado	86
On being alone by Aisling Tempany	87
The Sewing Class by Aisling Tempany	88
Question by Aisling Tempany	89
Beyond the KT Boundary by David Batten	90
Colonist by David Batten	91
A Fractured Self by Eithne Nightingale	92
Mother's Last Christmas by Chris Considine	96
Wonder by Marcus Smith	97
Pilgrimage to a Desert by Marcus Smith	98
Fugue with Her Ancestors by Marcus Smith	99
Domo to Geneva by Gabriel Griffin	100
The Singing Fish by Melanie Whipman	101
Mill Fever by Kaddy Benyon	109
Amongst Women by Kaddy Benyon	110
In Vitro Heuresis by Kaddy Benyon	111
Under the Bridge by Noel Williams	112
Domestic News by Noel Williams	113
Talisman by Noel Williams	114
Charlie Darling by MWS	115
Fukushima, Mile End by Alex Josephy	124
A New Beach by Alex Josephy	125
Dark Matter by Rosie Garland	126
Drinking the Water of the Nile by Rosie Garland	127
Accidental by Nicola Warwick	128
Homunculus by Nicola Warwick	129
The Reticulated Man by Nicola Warwick	130
Jericho by Vivian Hassan-Lambert	131
Flying by Karen Harvey	140
Migration by Karen Harvey	141
The umpteenth cycle by Jo Hemmant	142
The doctor say relax by Jo Hemmant	143
Symptomatic by Jo Hemmant	144
The gale blows itself out by Ian McEwan	145
Watch the birdie by Ian McEwan	148
Handsfree by Ian McEwan	149
Outpouring by Ian McEwan	150
Contributors	152

Jericho

Ten O'clock To Balham
Joanna Campbell

Amanda watched the guard pacing on the cold platform. Through the glass door's frosted ridges, he looked sawn-up into shifting vertical stripes. There was something comforting about his strutting gait, the flashes of blue uniform, the occasional shouts of greeting to regular passengers. He had promised to tell Amanda when she needed to return to the cold.

'No sense hanging about, love. Train's not due yet,' he'd said, his words were kind in the grating wind. 'You sit yourself down in the waiting-room. It's just for ladies, look. Nice for the babe to be in the warm. I'll give you a shout.'

Amanda wore a ring. Just a plain gold band like a curtain ring. Her parents had bought it from a catalogue.

'Gives a better impression,' they'd told her when she left this morning.

But Amanda didn't think the guard had looked at her finger. His eyes had met hers, glancing away to the track now and again through shyness or the need to check points and signals, or whatever guards did.

As he closed the door, Amanda felt the baby squirm. He was working up to overwhelming hunger. It might be less embarrassing to feed him here than on the train. She was alone at the moment.

She had just settled him at her breast when a woman appeared in the waiting room, setting her basket on the table. She sat opposite Amanda to watch, her head with its dandelion-clock hair tilted to one side. She didn't unfold a newspaper or examine her nails. She just beamed, creamy teeth prominent, pebble eyes on the baby's head.

Amanda glanced at the woman's black cape, then up at her mottled face. She smiled back and looked down again at the frantic mouth of her child. He pulled hard, as though this were his last feed on earth. Amanda curved her back into the plastic chair in the dreary room. The bar heater clicked.

Her parents had said, 'Call us Pamela and Derek. We're too young to be grandparents. Even 'Mum' and 'Dad' makes us feel old now.'

Their estate was full of thrusting nineteen-seventies couples, second and third bedrooms filled with files and holiday brochures.

They moved her into the back bedroom. They bought a record player and lava lamp to encourage her to stay in. Derek carved the baby's initials into the cot before he gave up whittling for squash. He walked out at feeding-times.

'Oh, can't you go out the back door with the pram?' Pamela had said as Amanda pushed it proudly off the front step. 'No need to flaunt it to the cul-de-sac.'

'I'm not flaunting. I'm proud.'

'But we have to live here, Amanda. With all the whispering. Let's be discreet, shall we?'

'Why bother? They must have already seen me looking enormous. What does it matter anyway? Don't you love your grandchild?'

'Of course! That's what I'm thinking of. We don't want them pointing and staring, do we?'

Amanda had reversed the pram. It felt like being six and told to face the corner.

When she left today, Amanda knew their cloak of parental concern was a shroud for their guilty glee at being Pamela and Derek again.

They offered her a lift. But the main line rumbled behind the tall beeches at the end of the back garden. Amanda felt the throb through the thin walls of her room. It pledged her release; beat out a message, a promise of acceptance from the outside world.

They slid the ring on her finger. It spun round, too large. She had to clench it in place.

Now she was baring her shame. Inviting the world to validate it. Turn it into a celebration instead of a cheerless secret. The world was waiting for her. Or at least Balham was.

She straightened her back and listened to the next announcement. She had a few minutes to unhook the baby and transfer him to the other side.

'It's good that you don't feel embarrassed. I do so admire you, you know. No need to hide in the Ladies when baby needs a feed, is there?'

Dandelion leaned on the table, peering closer. Amanda sweated and inched her chair back. An express blasted through the station. The woman's basket reverberated on the table.

She peeled off her cape. Underneath she was stout and starched in her nurse's uniform, dominating the room in her royal blue and white.

Amanda softened her shoulders and smiled again.

'How long before your train, dear?' The woman tightened her thick elastic belt. The ornate buckle glinted under the strip light.

'Only a few minutes unfortunately. He's so hungry he'll cry if I stop.'

'Got a good set of lungs has he?' The ivory grin was close. Amanda could smell Trebor mints; feel cold breath on her chest.

'Oh yes.'

They listened to the baby's gulping and swallowing, the popping electric fire.

'Does he take a bottle?'

'No. Well, I haven't tried yet. But I really have to. I've got a job in Balham.'

It was a relief to say it. Expressing milk had been a tense battle. An hour of pumping had produced a teaspoonful.

'I've got all the stuff, but I'm scared of making the break. You know, whether he'll be deprived of me…' She looked down at her pale-blue bag, engorged with teats and tubs.

The woman rustled over to Amanda's side of the table, blocking the light from the door.

'May I?' She gathered the equipment and assembled a bottle on the table.

'Unplug him, dear, while I get them to warm this in the café.'

Amanda sighed as she detached the baby. At last she would be free of wet circles on her blouse. She could pass him and his blue bag to the crèche in Balham. She laid the baby on the table by the woman's basket while she dressed. He turned red instantly and drew up his legs. She waited for the screams as she buttoned her blouse and laid him back on her lap.

In the pause before the crying began, she felt the growing warmth of his head on her thighs. His curly fingers clenched. Amanda felt sick. She pictured him in the crèche, his tiny lips rooting for her, longing for his mother's scent, her voice, her arms. And she would be trapped in a typing pool, lipstick on, lumpy chest still inflating, counting the hours until his head was tucked in the crook of her arm again. Would he know her?

The train rushed into the station as he roared.

She picked him up and laid his furious face against her neck.

He yelled into her soul.

The guard opened the door as the train rumbled to a standstill.

'Isn't this your train love? Want a hand?' His hair flopped onto his red face and his trousers were too short for his legs.

Tears tugged her eyes.

She buried her face in the baby's cardigan, inhaling the garden air.

'All right love?'

'She will be, won't you dear?' The dandelion hair appeared over the guard's shoulder. He looked relieved.

'I'll leave her in your capable hands then, Nurse. But she's not got long before it goes.'

He closed the door.

'Better keep the heat in, love.'

But Amanda could feel the bitter cold, even though a patch on her right leg was scorched by the red-hot bars of the fire.

The woman crouched, her eyes at the same level as the baby.

'I'll take him, dear. If a stranger does the first bottle, it's easier. If he smells Mum, he'll want the breast.' She screwed up her mouth, as if the thought left a nasty taste.

Amanda held on to the baby. A whistle screeched. Train doors slammed.

The woman's thumb-nails picked at her gilt buckle. 'Hundreds of mothers have passed their babies to me, dear. Trusted me. I know we've never met, but I love all babies. Lost three of my own, you see. All born blue.'

She smoothed her pinafore and held out her arms.

Amanda let the woman prise the baby off her soaking neck. In seconds he was rasping against the starchy royal-blue and white, his mouth full of rubber teat and the room filled with new sucking sounds.

Amanda heard a longer whistle and saw the cut-up strips of the gangling guard in the glass panel of the door.

'I have to go now.'

'You sort out your bags, dear, and get them on the train. I'll follow with the baby.'

Amanda picked up her holdall. She would miss the train if she didn't hurry.

'Leave the baby's bag. I can manage that.'

It was a command.

Amanda moved to the door. She had to let others take over

now. She'd told herself that. She put her hand on the door handle, then stopped. The guard would help her get on the train. She didn't need the woman now.

But she couldn't be rude. The poor thing had lost her own. Let her have one last minute. After all, Amanda's new life wouldn't begin in Balham. It had begun when she left home by the front door. She was in it now.

She turned back and saw the woman's basket on the table. It was empty, apart from a soft blanket printed with orange ducks, the corner turned back.

'All aboard!'

The guard opened the door an inch and called through.

'It's off any second, love. Are you going or not?'

He bounded back to the platform, leaving the door ajar.

Amanda hesitated. Took one step. She imagined her baby lying in that basket. Covered with the orange ducks. And she thought about being free and flat-chested again in Balham. And sleeping all night long. She took another step.

The guard dashed past. She saw him in the inch-wide gap, then streaking along the glass again, panicking about the time. She stood still, the sound of her child's breathing stifled by the train's engine.

'Come on, New Mum! Still going to Balham?'

She could see the guard properly now. He paused to give her a beckoning wave. Then he cupped his long awkward fingers under a old lady's elbow to help her up the step and into her carriage. Like a shepherd with his flock.

He came back for the last time. She could see every spot on his chin.

'New Mum, Balham train's going!'

'Yes, I'm coming. Can you give me a hand please?'

Amanda turned back to take her child.

'Thought that old girl was with you,' he said on the platform, his red wrists poking out from his cuffs as he took her bags.

'No, I don't know her at all.'

'My Mum's a nurse too. But they told her to give up wearing that big buckle thing. Carried germs, see. Haven't worn them for years now. They have quite a modern sort of uniform these days. Drip-dry and that.'

Amanda looked back. The nurse had vanished.

'Well, here's a nice empty carriage, love. '

He let her settle with the baby while he stowed her bags under the seat.

'There you go, love. Blimey, it's brass monkeys today.' He tucked in the trailing ends of the baby's shawl. 'I hope you've got a warm home to go to.'

He gave her a wink and closed the door.

Through the grimy window Amanda could read his lips.

'Make sure you get someone in Balham to help when you get off!'

She smiled and nodded, shifted the weight of the baby until they both sat in comfort. An elderly lady clucked at him, unable to resist smiling at his newness, his innocence, his purity.

Amanda let the ring slide off into her bag. The old lady smiled and clucked. She would clearly continue for the entire journey.

The engine was straining, desperate to begin. Amanda clutched her baby, relieved to feel its pressure against her breast, now tense with new milk. The train moved. The brakes released. How close she'd come to missing it.

Lindsey Holland

Urashima

You try to be a colour when the weather is greyscale.
Eyes search the ceiling. More new cracks.
You once said you saw beasts in the plaster.

In the apartment next door, Mr. Rodgers is whistling.
Your hands are a galaxy of gloss paint, and tubs
of one-coat wait by the cupboard—he's old and so

you won't take payment. The window shakes itself
and the lamp's reflection is a bonfire on a black hill,
someone else's land and endeavour while here

its light is a painful stroking like the thought of sex.
She'll come like a goddess through the rain. You'll let
the decades slip around her like smoke.

Beowulf

would have done the same. You spent weeks
in net cafes where the cockroaches swarm
under linoleum, in places where the word
blood is mentioned more than cappuccino.

I've followed you in hashtags, an avatar
of half a face and a blurred shoulder, not enough,
but your skin is lustre. An eyebrow spears
the border with its napped obsidian;

and this is how you planned, from the corners
where sand and dust are swept by alchemists
who turn it to rice, and the edges where
whispers travel fast along bastions.

You knew, before you could reach the palace,
with its gold and gems and private cinema,
that breath would stop, that the beast would launch
bottles of flame and spit its tear gas,

that tents and banners would beg translation
in the way that swords are more than metal,
that to cut the heart of that armoured belly,
you'd need, more than anything, a tongue.

Sigurd and Fafnir

Even though your brother was a junkie,
    took everything,
        (your mother sold her wedding ring and they
                defaulted)
        I'm still not sure
you should have tracked him to the farm
        where hay
            bales are a wall around a cloistered room,
                and sheathed
        steel is warmed
by a choler imbalance. If it were me
    my bowels
        would've fallen at the first voice, or maybe when
        that stone scout
            skittered its messages.
But then again, I wouldn't know where
    to buy a converted
        Baikel 8mm. Did the credits roll
                when you drew it,
        when their pit bull
muscles pulled back, when your tongue
    made real moment of
        Give me the fucking money? Dark echoes
        will hammer
           their curses
in your children's dreams. And though
    you'll stamp
        each serpent memory, they'll slip between
      the gaps
        in your teeth.

Edward Ragg

Waiver

If there is an art
Of emendation,

It is not in love
With the corrected

Proof, but the insistent
Gift of the unwritten.

How the leaves fall
Now to the wind's

Signature, how the eye
Of the wavering line

Glimpses these
Shadowed blacks

Of red, disclaiming
Everything except

The excusable clauses
Of the given.

The Entire Scale

The impossibility of the city
And globe and the outer
Reaches of that globe,

The dull pulse of entirety…
How tempting to say
Each life implies

An artistry in the
Rear of the actual,
How definitive.

The orange leaves
And the brown leaves
Courting in the square…

They define a force
That is spent or
Ebbing in the wind.

The winding towers,
The atelier and the rent
Scale in the pay of things,

Lyric tokens of an
Autumnal exchange.
Pianist and typist, too,

Are almost seasonal
Creatures, as much a man
Or woman rehearsing

How the afternoon becomes
Darker, how the music sounds
In love with the memory of light.

The Taking of the Capital

That first winter,
Three days of rockets
And fire-crackers

As if the sky was lit
With the nomenclature
Of the vivid;

Or the city taken siege
By aerial bombardments
Of light, sound and

Distance—for which
There are no names.
Then the odd incendiary

At the periphery of
Observance, as if a
Skulking spirit had

Tip-toed on the comedy
Of ritual combustion
Blown out in sound.

Such an offering has
Taken the look of things
From what we thought,

In the cinders of a capital
Which is not ours nor theirs
In the incense-heavy air.

Afterwords

How bright the shopping malls
In the softest December light

Descending, the simulacra
Of novelty…

Here aspiration and circumstance
Meet unravelling the lyrical

And convenience goods
And I have met them

Waiting for the words
That attend their conventions

In predictable lines…
What office I have

Is not at the calling stations
Nor between them really—

Valedictory voices in the
Corridors trailing—but

As aftersense before
The novelty of simulacra.

How the applicable words
In the softest December light

Ascending will unravel
Along less predictable lines

In the bright light where we will
Find them most conveniently.

Gemma Green

Exhibition

Anticipating jungle yellow and Tahiti green,
I watch the rain collect in the flagstones.
A toddler presses his face to the window,
underwater breathing to the outside world.
I toy with coffee and paper-cup soup
while the Thames belts its passengers through;
sodden tourists on pleasure cruisers,
with fluorescent hoods and wind-blurred faces.
Dividing us, a string of heaving trees
which if Gauguin had painted them
would rise from the canvas like fresh red hearts.

Hertz

Avignon, two cases, a week's life in each
heavy as gravestones, leaned in reception.
The girl from Hertz smiles to greet us
hers is the first face I see in France.
Teasing her colleague in broken English,
she draws a map of the railway station;
I catch the scars dappling her forearms
silvering thin and almost translucent.
That night in bed in the shuttered air,
I anxiously search the World Service,
hearing the radio slip between waves.
I think of my stretch marks, weight of a baby;
her paring her skin somewhere beyond this
carving crescents, olive leaves and heart traces.

Frances Corkey Thompson

Afternoon Telly

Classical sculptors, when they made a slip—
chipped, say, a regal cheek, would smooth in a fingertip
of beeswax, soothe and powder with marble dust,
polish to perfection

or almost. Your leg's long cut is healing, not yet healed.
They're telling us that a flawless work, one without wax,
is called *sin cera*, sincere. Through a day and then a night
in High-Dependency, I cushioned

your hushed white foot until the beat gurgled back
and ankle, instep and finally all five toes glowed roseate
and they took you away to the makers of bypass and artery.
Sincerity felt cold, my love. I'll hold the old

imperfect push and pull.

High
Jacqueline Haskell

Sometimes when he's on the wire, he forgets to breathe.

He carries it locked inside him until he starts to choke and gasp, as if the air itself is thin, and then he exhales, and the very motion of exhaling tips him off, sends him stiff and stumbling onto the grass.

He finds he often can't get back on when this happens, spends minutes circling the trees, sidling up to the challenge, rubbing his hands on their bark; then he steps over the wire, inspects it, circles again, again.

And as he circles he thinks about the early morning park people; people who keep him from *his* space, *his* trees.

The dog walkers with their grab-balls and their scoopers; the elderly lady in black doing Tai Chi; the homeless man pushing three supermarket trolleys to and fro from the toilets to the skateboard alley; a power walker in a yellow helmet—no joggers, it's not that kind of park; the grounds-man litter-picking, moving on to set a row of sprinklers on the bowling green (Rinks: Strictly Members Only).

People surround him; jostle him; crowd him; pour thoughts into his brain.

Don't get too close to me! He warns, and the words hover in his lungs, his breath suspended there, silent.

Right now there's a man on the park bench—the one tucked beneath the elms by the railings, less than an arm span away; he comes each morning, before six, and takes up the same position, lying on the narrow wooden slats, head immersed in the dim green of the shrubbery. He's never seen this man's face, close as he is, often doesn't even see him arrive—he's too busy practising—but when he turns, the dark wood of the bench has become the faded khaki silhouette of the man, knees bent, soles of half-decent boots turned out to face the world.

He knows that make of boot: knows how it will smell when lifted to be brushed and oiled; he can still feel the ingrained crease of worn leather.

He wonders if this man is like him, but he would never approach, never ask.

Don't get too close to me!

In all, he finds it unsatisfactory, these early mornings: there's too much distraction, too much purpose, too much movement, glimpsed from the corner of his eye.

Even the white birds that wheel down from the cliffs, their black heads crying and calling, even these birds seem jittery, glad to be away from the hostile, heaving sea, bringing something of the violence of its summer storms on their wing.

Don't get too close to Vallon man!

So he changes to the evening. It is high summer, so this is possible, will be for several months at least. And then, who knows? Well, he might just have it perfected by then...

In the evening it *is* better: a softer, kinder, quieter park. On warm nights couples sprawl on the grassy bank behind the flats, limbs pressing in on each other, on their vodka-increased attraction; the skateboarders thinning, discouraged by the shadows, drawn to the chance of a spot of underage drinking in the seafront shelter. A mate works at the local offie, he's heard: a mate who nods and winks at the smudge of their fake ID's.

He sets up, between his two trees, their trunks just rough enough to hold the line, rubbing the bark with the tension of his knots, until it is stripped back, chestnut coloured, gleaming.

He knows you should balance with a pole, but he's no money for one right now—he's living on his discharge pension; the practice wire came from Ritzi, who owns the café on the corner, but who used to come and go with the county fair, perform there, back when. A good all-rounder, or so he claims.

'Don't look down!' commands Ritzi, when he comes to see how he's doing. 'Nothing fancy, right? No tricks in the air: just get from A to B—one straight line!'

Not so hard then.
Don't look down!
Look down!
Look down! Fuck it boy, look down!

On the dark road, the Buffalo's spotlights cast a wide bright apron behind its flotilla of smaller escorts; its armoured snouts blow hot air at the heaps of rubbish and debris lining the desert route, looking for something different from the night before, and the night before that, and the one before it.

They salvaged the Buffalo from the Americans after it survived with its cabin intact when an IED took off the two front wheels, leaving its axle only *slightly bent, the run-flat tyres almost at their limit—only one more tour left in them, he reckons.*

He hears the wild dogs, packs of them, baying, startled by the light and the rattle of the Buffalo's chassis.

He gets out of the vehicle.

They told him it was only to be expected —considered normal even—this sense of *displacement*, as they called it—though he's no idea what that means—this sense of being dislodged from a task, bewildered; yes, that's better, he understands that alright, understands that it is when he is no longer hyped, no longer high on what he's trained for, when he is no longer out there, on the line, just inches from the IED's, that he will fear them most.

Some nights he even sits it out altogether, this new challenge, this task; he sets up, spreads out his anorak, the blue quilting already ingrained with dirt from the browned grass—scorched thin by an early summer heat wave, a hot, dry wind from the south—and then he lays down, with difficulty, his leg muscles won't yet bend, down beneath the wire so he can stare up at it, let it cut him, should it fall.

Tonight is one such night.

As he stares, he wonders what he'd hoped for from this war, from his part in it. What he'd hoped for after uni—the city like his mates? His life contained in plastic cubicles? What could he hope for still? What *outcome* might he dream of? What might yet still be possible? Even with this leg.

This feeling that he's been left wanting, that he's missing something—but that he himself has not been missed—has become another skin, a second membrane.

Displacement. Yes, if this is it, he feels it keenly.

The feel of the Vallon as he walks—not light, not heavy, just there, an extension to his hand. Metal seeking metal.

He remembers… he remembers, what, exactly?

But he can't remember, or at least not enough, not clearly: that's the problem.

Don't get too close to Vallon man – if he goes up…

Lying under the wire, he mentally rehearses—this is as good as the real thing, they say—better even—working it through in your mind, seeing each step, each detail, until you find the bomb, trip the wire.

Find the outcome you desire.

Don't get too close to Vallon man—if he goes up, you'll go with him!

He dreams of leaping from the tightrope wire: a taut springy wire, high in the sky—not the slack-sloped practice wire—and performing dizzying feats of daring; he dreams of being up there, where the air is thin.

He dreams he leaps, scissoring the wire—a perfect wire, a perfect leap—and catching it unawares, he tames it, this wire: a wild horse of tensioned steel.

And then he's back, for real this time; starting in the middle, where it's lower, running it between his big toe and his second toe, right to the centre of his heel.

He swings his good leg first, as he's been shown in physio, after the *revision surgery*, as they called it, to deal with the soft tissue damage and the muscle wastage.

Always your good leg first, lad—until you find your balance!

Of course, there were other, more obvious, activities; other activities he could have chosen—activities suggested in bold type on the list they gave him, all requiring the necessary concentration, focus, but none appealed. He liked to think he'd more imagination than that. And the gym had lost its lure: the sudden quiet in the changing rooms when he pulled off his shorts. The sight of his own thigh; the shower…

All around him, the night skims the trees, shortens them, blurs their leaves. But he sees only the wire, up front, up ahead of him. Always the wire.

And miraculously, this time he does it: he stays on, right to the end, hugging the tree with relief as he reaches the other side.

'Don't look back!' commands Ritzi sternly, on such occasions, though he's clearly proud of his protégé.

He too thinks he's doing rather well: he's come a long way since the flailing windmill arms of his first few attempts—might even be ready for the big day! It's only his daughter's sports fundraiser, weeks off at the start of the new school year, but with things the way they are with Jeanie—she hardly ever lets him see the kid—it's a chance. And it's only the parents' star turns, the silly part of the day, the light relief, but even so… even so, it's something…

Encouraged, he starts over at his task, tries to imagine the pole he can't afford: how it might feel in his hands, the weight of it—

not light, but not heavy either.

The first step.

He thinks back to that first step in rehab.

The white-jacketed physio.

The opioid therapy.

White pills, white noise, white dream.

White room.

No battalion here, in the shrivelled-green of the park; no praise for Vallon man and his fortitude and courage on point. No high risk areas; no white dust and partial detonation.

Just rehab and its opioids.

Rittle-rattling in his head, the pills. He has them somewhere still.

Rittle-rattle, like the schoolgirls with their cough sweets: girls who hang upside down on the bucket swings in the kiddies playground opposite, every evening after class is out; he can see them now, a fluttering of brown cloth and limbs, like tiny sparrows—skirts foaming over their thighs, tossing back their heads with laughter, then righting themselves, sucking in their breath, sucking in those sweets to save from choking.

Those rittle-rattle cough sweets, rolling round their dainty teeth, saliva flowing: tins of those sweeties rittle-rattling around inside their metal pencil cases, sucking up their A-grade futures.

Tonight, they pass close to him—too close—as they leave the park, sending the hum of their chatter vibrating down his wire, satchels slap-slapping against their thighs, against the pleats of those brown uniforms.

One of the girls stops right by his tree.

'What you doing?' she says, and it's sharp, almost an accusation.

Her voice startles him and he tumbles off the wire, clutching at the tree trunk for support, scraping his knuckles on the flaking bark in his haste, his bad leg clumsy and awkward as it hits the ground.

He steadies himself, turns to face the girl.

She's shorter, younger even, rounder than the others, without that sudden spurt of growth that turns them thin and gangly. Her blond hair is streaked red and purple, knotted into plastic clips pulled high on her crown.

'Practising,' he says, after a moment.

'Yeah, right!' she says. 'Can't you walk or what?'

'It's a high wire,' he says.

'A what?' she asks, and for a second he thinks she's actually interested.

'A tightrope,' he says, '- like the circus.'

'But you're on the ground!' she says, making a small snorting sound through her nostrils. 'And your leg's all funny...'

'I'm just practising,' he says, helpless to describe it, the hum of his body on the wire, the feel of his limb.

'Want a sweet then do you?' she says, ignoring him and holding out her sweet tin. It's a small oval, pale green, with pictures of lady-bugs on the lid, a bright ladybug-cluster, a burst of red, and —for some reason he can't quite fathom, some connection he can't yet make—it puts him in mind of that last dismount.

The kids. He always talks to the kids, on dismounts. Foot patrols. Gives them whatever: pens, small change, sunglasses, and they beg whatever they see him carrying, whatever they fancy—and he's known for being soft: sometimes it's his watch or even a play with his weapon.

He'll stop to talk to one or two and then there'll be thirty, forty kids, swarming.

This time it's Asadabad, down a roadside canal running towards the operating base. Word comes that insurgents have been spotted, in the village.

He's clambering through the mouseholes, entering the compound: one of the NP's has seen a spate of rocket attacks, has called in the reaction task force.

His Senior Rifleman, the guys, all the guys, are behind him.

He watches as she opens the lid, easing it back with her shiny, star-filled nails, holding it out to him, waving it in his face. The sight of it makes him want to retch; he's been this way since the return—must have left his sweet tooth back in Kunar.

'Th...thanks, no,' he says, with a stammer he didn't know he had.

'Go on!' she says, pushing it closer, rattling it, taking a step towards him, then another. 'Cough drops, see!'

He wants to step back, to step away from her, but doesn't want the embarrassment, doesn't want her to see him stumble again.

He reaches out a hand, still hanging onto the tree with the other. He doesn't want to appear rude, even though he knows she's playing him.

'Wait up, mister!' she says and the tips of his fingers are almost touching the sweets when she jerks the tin away, and bringing it up to her lips she spits, sending her own saliva-sucked sweet scooting into the centre of the tin, where it sits round and shiny as a cherry stone.

He gets out of the vehicle.
They're all here, the kids, playing by the water. One of the girls comes over—one he knows by name—clutching the hem of her dress, hugging it to her like a cloak.

She'd been there a few weeks back when he'd gone to the District Centre and taken a bag of kite kits, helped the kids make them up, fly them. Something they hadn't been allowed to do when the insurgents ruled.

'Boom! Boom!' she's saying now, pointing back to the embankment, making wild explosive gestures with her free hand, the other lost in the folds of her skirt.

He goes over there, to the embankment, and finds a bundle of old mortar canisters hidden under a mound of hay—all of them empty, rusting, useless.

He walks back to her, smiling.

'Boom!' he says, giving her the battalion's fist bump greeting.

'It's alright!' he calls out, laughing as he waves the others through: the men, the vehicles. All the men. 'It's only Fareima! Just a kid!'

His rifleman moves forward, bends to offer the girl a sweet—a tiny candy in a striped cellophane wrapper—and he watches the girl twitching the hem of her dress, and he thinks she's going to reach out and take the sweet, but instead she starts pulling at the material, pulling out a pin from under it and hurling what—too late, much, much too late—he sees is the unmistakable dark-rugby-ball mass of a grenade…

Boom! A ground shock, and he's on his back, his weapon lost, arms flung wide…

Nearby, someone screaming. Later, they would tell him it was him.

Everything else silent, like a fall of snow.

His rifleman beside him, head lolling at an impossible angle, a sinew of blood and white bone. Grey matter.

'Boom!'

The men; the vehicles. All the men.

Fareima.

Just a kid.

The blond girl looks at him, running her purple-stained tongue slowly round the rim of her lips, as if there's some residue, some stickiness there, and then she steps back, snapping shut the tin and tossing it into the open pocket of her satchel and she takes off, her plump legs kicking out each side of her.

'Spazzo!' she calls back at him, over her shoulder.

'C'mon, Trace!' yells one of the other girls.

'Yeah, let's get chips!' calls another. 'You're paying!'

He can hear the snickers behind him, erupting into whoops of laughter.

Nearby, someone screaming.

Later, they would tell him it was him.

Sometimes when he's on the wire, he forgets to breathe.

But this time he inhales, keeping what air he can inside him, and then he takes that first fine glorious step.

Beneath him the crowd is still, holding its collective spectator-breath, astounded into submission.

Gripping the line between his toes—the toes of both his legs—he springs to dizzying heights, high above the mown grass of the sports field; a perfect leap, away from the armoured ironclaw with its thick-lensed portals, away from the baying dogs and the heaps of desert debris and the blank-faced man and the crying birds; away from the little rittle-rattle girl with her tiny lady-bug candy in its striped cellophane wrap; riding the wire, heading out onto the line, up where the air is thin.

Martin Willitts Jr

The Female Snowy Owl

It is on the branch of the night sky
in the snow-crush.
It makes a *krek* before it lifts its brown feathers.

This is how you notice death before you see it.
You cannot move fast enough
even if you have a warning.
It moves faster than you can react.
It is gone before sound is gone.

We all need warnings; but we never get them.
We all try to blend into our environment.
It is survival. It is paying attention,
swivelling our heads to see everything.

Their song is a deep repeated *gawh*.
They click their menacing tongue.

What warnings, if any, do we give?
What whiteness do we bring?
This is how they exist; what is our excuse?

Our footprints in snow, snap—a cocked trigger.

The Snow Queen
Based on *The Snow Queen* by Hans Christian Andersen

I loved grooming your hair, smooth as new snow;
now nothing of you remains with me.
You have left me.
The weight of loss curses through my blue skin.
You've shattered my icy heart.

You gave me cold stares.
I should have known then, you would not stay.
Again, when your eyes were geese heading north,
I should have seen the change of weather in your sighs.
You never spoke my name after that.
That too, was a clue.

I was a lover always hoping for a second chance,
hoping frantically against frozen wisdom,
remembering only the good parts of a fairy tale romance.
I had not expected much
and I got exactly what I had expected.

This is what I hoped for:
someone to listen to my long wintry stories;
someone to bray like a timber wolf when I was missing;
a few crumbs of conversation like snowshoes
in the whistle of tree pines.
Love should be a blizzard of falling stars;
not the nightmares of snowed-in villages.

You gave me nothing.
You barely could whisper my name without contempt,
and even then you spoke coldly.
Your love was like catching small glimpses of spring.

I will not chase after you.
You are simply not worth it.
My life is so many curses as it is.

There will be others after you.
There always are.

Jill Teague

Hare's Madness

I brook no foolish burrowing in the dark,
born with both eyes wide open.
My split lip dribbled milk,
a warm gift from a dam's soft belly.

I weave through waves of corn,
tread the cropped stalks
like smouldering coals.
Only the fleet of heart may catch my drift.

My thigh is iron.
I wrench forked mandrake shrieking
from the earth. I sense the tensing of a talon
before the brain of hawk believes its eye.

Still as a druid stone I sit
as the moon out stares her own distraction.
I walk on water of my own conviction.

War Paint

I remember your stories
told only to me
in the darkness we shared
before sleep.
Of souls
loving the untamed land,
of feather and bones,
and paint
made from the earth.

I dreamed then,
of wild places, of horses
the colour of prairie rainbows,
a line of warriors
joining earth with sky.

The circle of years
brought us to barren land.
Backed into corners we fought,
rattling like empty pods,
war paint dripping in the blaze
of an angry sun.

Returning home
after your sudden death,
you had left one moccasin
lying in the dark.
I wept then for the endings
I would miss,
and the shared wild places
of our separate hearts.

David Ford

Looking Over Strange Terrain

I wanted a thick Nantucket fog
to roll beneath the door
and envelope us like two rings
in purest cotton wool.

You gave me what I wanted.
Sometimes the tips of our bare
fingers touch but mostly we
cannot find each other

and only the occasional muffled clink
of metal tells us we are still looking.

Man and boy in a mirror

The boat has been sunk,
a lightbulb parachutes from the ceiling,
the stiff corpse of a toothbrush
on the edge of the sink.
He is a polarhund, teeth bared,
his hand forever on your shoulder.
The war is not over yet.
He pulls the tie tight, then tighter.
The soap grenade fizzes in the bath.

Lily and The Blue Book
Lindsey Stanberry-Flynn

Lily sat down on the bench and felt the slats hard against her thighs. Taking her lunch box from her bag, she placed it on the seat beside her. The wind bit into her shoulders and the branches of the huge willow sweeping down to the lake lifted and danced. She felt cold air wrap itself round her cheeks. This was her favourite time of year. Its rituals—scuffing through leaves, buttery crumpets, the glitter of sparklers—a last link with her mother.

Lily sensed movement, felt a thud on the bench. She screwed up her eyes—if she didn't look, they couldn't be there. She was used to averted faces, dark corners, silences. Then she smelt it. A stale, acrid smell. She risked a sideways look. A hand, raised blue veins striping its back, nails curling at the tips, was reaching towards her lunch box. The hand pounced and, like a wicked giant kidnapping a helpless baby, grasped one of the sandwiches. Her eyes fixed on the hand as it travelled to its owner's mouth.

'Hey! That's mine,' she said. The sandwich disappeared. She watched the mouth chewing inside its grizzled beard. Her eyes raked over the yellow-white hair, the trousers torn at the knee, coat tied together with string. As she stared, the figure at the other end of the bench reached out and grabbed a second sandwich.

Lily snatched up the lunch box with its remaining triangles of bread and shoved it into her bag. 'How dare you?' She forced her voice louder than she'd heard it for a long time.

The tramp stared ahead. What was he looking at? Please don't let it be the lake—or worse, her glorious willow. Lily followed the line of his gaze. Something had gone wrong: the willow was different. The feathery branches twitched against the water in the wind and the tree had cast a black shadow on the patch of grass in front of her. She made herself turn back to the tramp.

He was chewing steadily, and then he drew a hand across his mouth. Her eyes flicked from the nails to the beard: a storybook wizard, but no magic was going to come from this—*thing*.

He seemed oblivious of her, as he delved into one of his pockets and pulled out a book. A book? A knife, a bottle, pickings from other people's lunches—any of those wouldn't have surprised her, but a book! He opened it and began to read.

The pulse in Lily's temple throbbed. 'You ate my sandwiches!' She knew she sounded ridiculous.

The tramp put his finger on the page and leaned towards her. His skin was parchment pale and his eyes were thinly blue, like the early morning sky. It was not at all the face she was expecting.

'I prefer white bread,' he said, 'and thicker slices.' The voice was smooth and cultured. And there was something distinctive about it... that slow delivery, the thickening of the 'r' sound... 'And I'm not overly keen on smoked salmon.'

A flash caught Lily's eye. A crow swooped on to the grass in front of her, the green sheen of its feathers glinting through the menace of its blackness. It hopped a few steps, and it was then she noticed the twitching mass beneath it. It had caught a baby bird and was tearing at its flesh and feathers.

She rounded on the tramp. 'Didn't stop you eating it!'

The finger was still poised on the page. 'You can't beat a mature cheddar to my mind.'

Every bit of Lily craved escape. Anywhere, as long she could be free of this... this... monster, with his arrogance, his cheek, his poisonous smell. Her feet wriggled inside her boots. But why should she run away? Let him win? She'd done nothing wrong.

Her eyes returned to the lake: its surface rippled in the wind. The branches of the willow dipped and swayed. She imagined her limbs, reaching, stretching, tension easing out of her with the movement. It was no good getting worked up. *You know it doesn't do you any good*, Granny's voice sounded in her head. She pictured the outrage that was thrashing about inside her; she pushed at it, moulded it until it was a size she could manage. Then she shut it in a box, snapped the lid shut.

She sucked the cold air into her lungs. Perhaps he'd respond to reason. In his world it might be okay to help yourself to what you wanted, but it wasn't right. Surely he must see that. She turned to face him again.

The other end of the bench was empty. She'd only glanced away for a few seconds, but the tramp was gone. She scoured the path to the park entrance. A child on a bike, a woman pushing a pram, the park keeper sweeping leaves. No sign of him. She checked in the other direction. He couldn't have gone that way—she'd been gazing at the lake and he'd have had to walk past her.

Lily let the bag with the remains of lunch fall to her lap. She dabbed at the mark left on her jacket. She still had a banana, but she wasn't hungry any more. Her mouth felt gritty, as if she'd been swallowing sand. Everything seemed the same as when she'd arrived at the bench—the trembling lake, the swaying willow—they were still there. Yet her bench no longer felt secure. The tramp had tainted it.

As she stood up, she glowered at the spot where the tramp had sat, wishing she could erase his impact. There, at the far end of the bench, lay a blue rectangular shape. She picked it up. It was the book the tramp had been reading. She turned it over and read the gold lettering on its cover: *The Collected Works of J. Walter Matthews*. J. Walter Matthews? She couldn't recall hearing the name before. Her fingers caressed the cover's soft leather, the embossed letters of the title.

She opened the book—words, phrases jumped out at her: *autumn's russet hues... the darkness of the blackbird's silence... love's dread departure*. At school she had learnt loads of poetry by heart, but these words didn't chime with any memories.

She turned back to the title page, searching for a date. She couldn't see one, but underneath the title, in an ornate script, she read the flourish of a signature: J.Walter Matthews. The book looked old. It might be worth something with that signature. Perhaps she should hand it in at the police station. She peered to right and left. Probably the tramp had realised by now. Would appear along the path at any second. Would catch her with the book, *his* book in her hands. Without giving herself time to think, she replaced the book at the end of the bench and turned away.

She counted her paces: ten to where the path intersected another one; five to the toddlers' play area; fifteen more and she would arrive at the flowerbeds, cleared and empty for winter, the earth newly-turned and mine-black. As she reached a wheelbarrow piled high with dead chrysanthemums, the wind gusted, giving the wasted blooms momentary life. It tugged at her hair, the collar of her jacket, her sleeve, like a spiteful child.

No, she couldn't leave the book there. Anyone might come along and pick it up. Someone who didn't know it belonged to the tramp; someone who might sell it and pocket the money. Of course, it was obvious what to do. She'd leave a note: *Book safe. Taken to library.*

Shielding her eyes against the slanting sun, she picked out the bench. There was someone sitting there. Had he come back? She squinted into the light. No, there were two figures, younger, dark haired. She retraced her steps.

A boy and girl, about seventeen or eighteen, were sitting on the bench, her head on his shoulder, their hands entwined. She was holding the book and reading from it. Lily could just hear the words: *As the sun dies, and the clouds muster, your footsteps ring out on the scarred stones...* The boy barked out a laugh: 'Load of crap!'

Fear nipped at Lily as she drew close to the boy and girl: the crested raven-coloured hair, watchful eyes ringed with black, black leather coats, black boots. But she had to say something—the girl was bending the cover back. 'That's mine.'

The girl glared up at her. 'Who you talking to?'

'I'm sorry... the book's mine... well, not mine exactly...' Lily heard her voice trail away.

The girl looked at the book and then back at Lily. She laughed and a gold stud in her tongue shone dangerously. 'What you reckon?' she said to the boy.

He flicked his middle finger several times against the cover, the noise like a putter of rifle fire. 'Chuck it.'

The girl hesitated. Lily felt the pain of her nails digging in to her palms. Tears weren't pushing at the back of her eyes. Her legs weren't trembling. They weren't. She wouldn't let them.

The girl seemed to make up her mind. She opened the book wider, and flung it away from her. It hovered in the air above Lily. Then landed beyond the path and settled, splayed on the grass.

Lily darted forward and seized it. She turned to walk away. The laughter of the boy and girl faded.

By the time Lily got back to the library, Alison was waiting, her coat already flung over her shoulders.

'Where on earth have you been? You've messed up all the lunch breaks.'

Lily clutched the poetry book tighter. 'I'm sorry.'

'Foxy says there's a load of returns waiting to be shelved.'

Lily stared at Alison's pearly-white teeth, just visible between her glossy lips. She was always so certain.

'There was a man... a tramp... in the park—'

Alison's eyes darkened. 'What? He didn't... do anything, did he?'

'He ate my sandwiches.'

Alison grinned at her. 'Oh God! You had me going there for a minute.'

Lily held out the book. 'He left this behind.'

Alison ran her hand over the dark blue leather. 'J. Walter Matthews.'

'Have you heard of him?'

Alison took the book and flicked through a few pages. 'Nope.'

Lily watched Alison's face as she turned to the title page. She saw her lips purse.

'A signed copy. Not worth as much with a signature.'

'But the tramp could still sell it. Buy himself some comforts.'

'Perhaps he's happy as he is.'

'Dirty? Hungry? He can't be.' Lily pulled the book from Alison. 'I mean... he didn't even sound like a tramp. Something terrible must have happened to make him live like that.'

'But at least he's free.' Alison's teeth gleamed. 'Not like us. Doesn't have to put up with Foxy's petty rules and regulations.'

When Lily got home Granny and Granddad were in the kitchen. He was sitting at the table reading his paper; she was at the stove, stirring something in a saucepan. Of course they were often busy doing other things. Granny loved her flowers and spent hours in the garden; she sewed and did voluntary work at the hospice shop. Granddad carved wooden toys and shavings of pine would attach themselves to his brown corduroys. But in Lily's mind, Granny was always at the stove, Radio 4 chattering in the background, and Granddad was always reading the paper. A tableau that hovered in her consciousness, along with half-formed images: wreaths of steam in the bathroom... a gold necklace... a car, red as tomato ketchup, its top open, and Mummy waving up at the window.

Granddad looked up with a smile. 'Hello, Dilly-Dilly. How are you?'

Lily crossed the room and kissed the top of his head. His forehead was ridged with lines.

'How was today?' he asked.

A picture of the tramp, his poetry book now pushed deep inside her bag, collided with the memory of the black-rimmed eyes of the boy and girl. 'Fine,' she said. 'It was fine.' She looked towards Granny, whose back in its grey cardigan was set firmly against the room. She turned to Granddad and saw the warning in his eyes. She ventured closer. The fibres of the cardigan seemed to tighten as if they sensed her drawing near. 'Hello, Granny.'

'You're late.'

'I had to stay on at the library. Alison went home sick.' Granny hated lies, but better that than reveal she had to make up the time because she was late back from lunch.

'You know how I worry.'

Lily stared at the bloated knuckles of Granny's arthritic fingers. 'Sorry.'

'Sorry. Sorry. Everyone's sorry.'

'What time's tea, Freda, love?' Granddad called out.

Granny glared over her shoulder at him, waving her spoon in his direction. 'The same time as last night and the night before.'

Granddad folded his newspaper and stood up. 'Time for a quick game of scrabble first, Dilly-Dilly?'

'I wish you wouldn't call her that!' Granny snapped. 'How many times have I told you?'

Granddad winked at Lily. *Lavender's blue, Dilly Dilly, lavender's green, When I am king, Dilly Dilly, you shall be queen.* His deep bass voice filled the kitchen.

Granny's spoon whirled round the saucepan. 'Dilly Doolally more like.'

Lily followed Granddad into the living room. She watched as he set out the scrabble board, counted out seven letters for each of them. Black hairs curled along the side of his hand and across the base of his fingers.

Once, a long time ago, it snowed and on the way back from school, there was a snowball fight. She must have been about eight, because she could still remember her mother clearly. Her father had gone away when she was a baby and she couldn't recall him at all, but back then she could remember her mother, the way she wrapped her in a warm towel after a bath; the letter she wrote to the tooth fairy when Lily's first tooth fell out; the feel of her hand when they skipped towards the swings in the park. That day, when it snowed, Lily had laughed. The noise coming out of her throat sounded strange, until she realised she was laughing. It was the first time since Mummy went. She opened her mouth and snowflakes landed on her tongue. She made a snowball and it hit one of the boys on the arm. He threw one back—it landed on her shoulder, the snow collapsing against the dark blue of her coat.

Granny had been waiting at the front door when she arrived. She pulled her into the house and slapped her hard across the legs. Lily felt the pain, even through her woolly tights.

She sat in her bedroom in the dark until Granddad came home from work. She heard the slam of the front door, the sound of raised voices in the kitchen, and then his feet on the stairs.

Lily rushed to him as soon as he opened her bedroom door and flung herself into his arms. His cheek was rough with bristles, and she rubbed her face against it, until it too was wet with her tears.

'There, there, Dilly-Dilly,' he crooned, the words a prickly whisper against her ear. 'Don't upset yourself.'

'Why does Granny hate me?' she sobbed.

'Hate you?' His voice sounded strange, she remembered, not with the usual chuckle gurgling through the words. He carried her over to the bed. 'Sit yourself, down there, love.' He threaded his fingers through hers and the black hairs along the side of his hand tickled. 'She doesn't hate you.' He seemed bewildered, like the lion in The Wizard of Oz. 'I think it's because you remind her,' he said at last.

'Of what?'

'Of your mummy. You're so like her, sometimes it's as if she was back with us. As if it had never happened.'

That night, when she'd had her bath and Granddad had read her a story and said goodnight, Granny came up to her room. She sat on the edge of the bed and in the light from the landing, Lily could make out the set of her mouth, the wrinkles round her eyes. She held her breath, waiting for Granny to speak. Instead, Granny leaned forward and pulled Lily towards her. Lily felt Granny's arms round her, small kisses landing on her forehead, her cheeks. She breathed in the warm scent of baking that Granny seemed to carry with her.

'Do you love me, Granny?' she asked, her face squashed against the silky material of Granny's blouse.

'Of course I do, my darling. More than life itself.'

Lily started to close her eyes, but then she heard Granny's voice again rumbling against her cheek. 'I just need you to be good. If you're good, then nothing bad can happen.'

Lily twists her head to the clock. The red digits glare at her—03:05. She pummels the pillow and flips it over, so that the cool side is against her cheek. She watches a beam of light slice across her curtained window, as a car passes in the street below. Her room springs to attention. Her dolls are perched on the chest of drawers—there's Dorothy after a great-aunt, Lauren from her first friend at nursery, and Lily, her favourite. *You can't call your dolly Lily. That's your name.* Someone had said that, she remembers, but whom? Granny? Or was the light tinkle of sound her mother's voice? A pile of jigsaws is stacked in the corner. Lily used to love jigsaws, finding the edge pieces first, the fact that each one had exactly the place where it belonged, the sense of completeness. Next to the bed are the bookshelves Granddad made for her. She helped him smooth the wood, rubbing with sandpaper after he'd worked on it with something called a plane. Her books are arranged in alphabetical order, but sometimes the different heights, the up and downness of them, like a mountain chain or a bucking sea, upsets her, and she has to change them round.

What on earth has she done? She should have left the poetry book where it was. Let it take its chance with the boy and girl. Why did she claim it? She even said—*that's mine*. Okay, she could argue that she rescued it for the tramp. But why has she brought it home?

Granny's maxim pounds in her head—*if you're good, nothing bad can happen*. Lily has been good. Passed her A levels, got the job at the library, keeps her room tidy, washes up… She even stopped asking questions about her mother, because Granny got that look. She's been good, so that nothing bad could happen. And now this. Somehow, she's stolen the book. Just the word makes her face burn.

She wouldn't go back to the park bench, she'd told herself: it was tainted, spoilt, poisoned, polluted—but how many days had she held out? Three? Four? And here she was. Her fingers touched the poetry book in the bag at her side; she opened the lunch box and placed it next to her. She'd made the sandwiches specially— mature cheddar with thick white bread. The green paint on the bench was still peeling; mothers were pushing babies; two boys kicked a ball. The branches of the willow dipped and swayed. And she waited.

On cue, the bench vibrated. She felt the tiny tremors of movement. She stared at the frothy branches of the willow tree; she stared at the rippling surface of the lake; she stared at the sky until its vast greyness seemed to invade her brain.

Then as if with a will of their own, her eyes swivelled to the side. Dark hair curling over his collar; a cream jacket; blue jeans; shiny brogues. Her chest began to ache and she realised she was holding her breath, pent up, waiting.

The man twisted on the bench to face her. 'You came back then?' It was a statement rather than a question.

'What do you mean?'

The brown eyes held hers. 'You came back. I've checked every lunchtime. I was sure you'd be back.'

It was the voice. That same voice.

She shifted away, closer to the end of the bench and felt the poetry book digging into her thigh. 'You're the tramp.'

'May I?' His hand was poised over the lunch box, his fingers reaching towards a sandwich. He lifted the top slice of bread. 'Ah, cheese. I'm touched you remembered.'

She watched him eat the sandwich and stretch out to take another. The flush reared up on her throat and warmed her cheeks. 'What do you want?' Her voice was high, demanding. She sounded like Granny.

He laughed then, his face all crinkly like wrapping paper. He held out his hand. 'I owe you an apology.'

His hand was warm and soft.

She pulled hers free. 'I don't know who you are,' she said, 'but I took your book. I know I shouldn't have, but there was this boy and—'

'It's okay. It's my fault, not yours.' There it was again, that soft burr of the 'r' sound. 'Let me explain.'

'You're not a tramp?'

He shook his head. 'Obviously my disguise was too good. I'm Robert Hudson, and I'm a psychologist. I'm writing a book about people's reactions to difficult or unexpected situations. You were one of my guinea pigs.'

'Are you allowed to do that—without people's permission?'

'Unlikely.' He spread his hands wide. 'My methods do sometimes get me into hot water.'

Lily let the air sigh out of her. She felt as if she'd been holding her breath ever since he'd sat down. 'What about the poetry book?' she said.

'That was a ploy—an old book, signed copy. All designed to make it seem valuable.'

Emotions whirled inside her, like leaves caught up in a gust of wind: she wasn't a thief, but he'd made a fool of her, testing her, waiting to see what she'd do; she wasn't a thief, but how dare he use her as a guinea pig?... 'So who is J. Walter Matthews?' she demanded.

'Some minor poet. I found the book in a second-hand shop.'

'A real person?'

'Most definitely.'

'Who signed it?'

He made a face. 'That was me. I do hope you'll accept my apology.'

She didn't answer.

'I didn't intend to upset you.'

'What about the experiment?' she asked. 'How do people react?'

The man shrugged. 'Too soon to say.' He stood up. 'But you were wonderful.'

'I was?'

'The way you stood up to that boy and girl.'

'You were watching?'

'I'm afraid I was. But I was so proud of you. You saved the book, and I'd like you to keep it to remind you how you stood up for something you believed in.' He gave a little bow. 'And I *love* your sandwiches.'

Lily sits in her bedroom, waiting for her grandmother's call. It's Tuesday evening, so it will be beef casserole for tea. Granny will talk about the daffodil bulbs she bought at the WI sale. Granddad will call her Dilly-Dilly, and Granny will frown. Afterwards, she and Granddad will wash up, while Granny listens to *The Archers*, and then Granny will sew while Granddad falls asleep in front of the television. The television will be too loud; the fire too hot. The phone might ring, and Granny will have one of her long, involved conversations. The call won't be for Lily.

She looks down at the book resting in her lap: *The Collected Works of J. Walter Matthews*. I didn't steal you after all, J. Walter Matthews. I saved you. And now I've got to save myself.

Phil Madden

The priest offers haircuts

With guilt in short demand the priest offers haircuts. Wrapped in the cloak customers feel invisible and tell all. 'Same as usual?' is enough to release stories of stoicism and despair. Also tales of immense trivia and tentative prejudice. He is used to these and listens with one hand.

If things go well he may retro diversify into surgery or at least sell certificates of cleansing. At close of day he mixes the cuttings into a magic compost of secrets. Unconstrained by confidentiality then, like history, he offers them to the highest bidder.

Origami Haiku

the origami
is not ready yet
at the moment it is only perfect

the envelope
contains itself

silence and sound
interunfold

in the bar I will open
my heart until
it is time to close

paper river's
paper boat
sails by paper stars

hot origami
wraps fish and chips

the origami
is in the gym
to get in better shape

do I have to guess
the shape of our love?

what began as a boat
became a bird.
Love is like that.

tonight cut out
the origami
just give me your hands

The Fox on the Moor

I see him just as he sees me.
Not knowing how he sees me.
Liquid freeze framed.
One way time truce.
Then he turns.
It would be fleeing if not for the shrug.
Vanishes into
an invisible hollow.
Deep inside me.
When the time is right,
he will hunt me out.

Anna Johnson

Dreamcatcher

Mirror shivers in the mass.

> Bound branches, dark cradle:
> a familytree hung with crushed foil.
> The twisting things wink and disappear
> to re-appear as half a silvered thought.

A blade.

> Hawthorn, pink and pale, spliced
> to a moon-weathered bone, a beetle
> tucked between the stamina, is dusted,
> covered, sleeping under snow.

A ring.

> A map-winged moth (*Hepialidae*)
> finds the sugar cube, proboscis
> touches the sweet rough, mouth-
> sap to a crystal for a night-sipped kiss,

a dit

> falls to the dark-wet grass.
> Navigating clouds of oiled air—
> lily, loveage, lavender—a rosemite
> lights on the lunar surface of a pearl.

A pin.

> The spider prints a tiny font
> on a mirror flinder, dewed glyphs
> of patient exploration. And inside the night
> the work is spun: laced, wound,

into a living wish.

Crucifix

He is bleeding on the Old Kent Road.
They are there at the front,
pens ready, mustard in the blood.

Ignominy—the end of failure—not being able
to help oneself in the end. No hands
help or bitter ones and cramped.

But they are keen—hands out for the crown—
seeing their names in the book,
made desperate by it. Miserere.

They want him to bleed *Go on then*
for the Rapporteur on the scene.
Guts and Glory. Shining. Vinegar on the wind.

Clare Dyer

Malta

Leaving Mdina we barely speak;
all that could be said has soaked

its high walls, its soft stone, been cast
wide across laced plains to the sea.

We'd dined; the sky caught
by orange trees, pressed

to the cut of rosemary, marjoram,
mint. We'd whispered small prayers

to the shadows of a hundred
doorway cats and, in the cathedral-quiet

the sun had hummed, had strummed.
And we came here to the hallelujah

of Sliema's evening streets: the snackle
of roof-top washing, the bell-peal

of Our Lady Star of the Sea, and this fiesta:
this bud and bloom of fireworks,

of dance; the beat between each flare
and roar as long as silence, as love.

Dowry (i)

I bring with me my grandfather's apples—
brushed with newsprint, fingers
and heat—packed with the tenderness of children,
wrapped as though made from glass. I bring
with me the engine hum of wasps
and windfalls, the quiet-cold earth;
his dugout, his shelter—its walls,
its cupped, dark air still heavy with war.
I bring with me the imprint of flowers,
of lime-scented grass; his stooped back,
a Spitfire sun in his hair. I bring with me
tang and core and seed, the blush of skin,
the silent season slip—
rain that beads and gathers like harvest.

Dowry (ii)

I give you the day my mother died, its winter slice;
lay it on the floor at your feet, ask you to shrine it
with me. There was the banded light, banding
through the call my father took; the seconds,
how they slowed and my hands and feet grew
vast—grew cosmic, immovable; how the walls
bred pinholes, pinholes to galaxies where she still lived.
There was vague clamour as we strained
to see, but, as we strained, they winked;
these galaxies winked, they disappeared.
I give you the quiet days after; to vacuum-wrap,
store in cupboards, in the corners
of our house; ask you to craft handles,
tenderly close the door.

Margaret Wilmot

The British Museum At 60

A calcite bowl from Ur contains
my parents and me and time, ur-time.
Dad's heart beat with a thousand eyes,
Mom loved Egypt—and me, I wished
I had my jump-rope in all the lovely museum space.
Thank-you, bowl.

The hands which made the bowl
happened upon a shape which would contain
whole civilizations, and me too, in one rounded space.
Art? Once upon a time
Dad's hands could wish
a lump of clay alive if they only used his eyes.

Not with your eyes,
Dad, but I like looking—at bowls,
the Rosetta Stone, marbles from the Parthenon. I wish
these were moments we could share. Life contains
so much that's poorly timed—
like death. Negative space.

Or maybe not—maybe it's that empty space
we need to truly see. I use my eyes
in a new way now. The times
I catch a glimpse in a mirror-bowl,
of jump-rope, pigtails, I wonder—me? The mind contains
its own museum, disparate bits I wish

I could connect, let go. I wish, I wish
upon a star. School groups throng. No space
for jump-ropes in museums now. Three kids can't contain
their snickers as they eye
a woman thrusting out a giant breast, then bowl
past me pointing at a stag. Not ten-year-olds but times

have changed, all kinds of time.
Tea in the Great Court, and wishing
for nothing beyond this moment. The huge glass bowl
above fills with clouds drifting across blue space,
joining like continents, rifting ... My eyes
dive as a small boy hurtles near, unable to contain

himself in all this lovely space. His mum contains
him on a stool, places a bowl before him, catches my eye.
We smile. Time. What can we wish?

Caryatid, *Modigliani*

By naming her *Caryatid*, the artist
suggests that the woman we see unfolding herself—
from sleep perhaps, waking in all simplicity
and stretching—will like so many women rise and assume
a world's weight: for what is this slant shape
across her shoulders but the base to
a wide vessel embracing shadow and chalky space?
A charcoal outline locates the supple form
on a front plane against blue strokes so broad, so light
we glimpse the naked paper as through a flimsy scrim. No marble,
no fluted columns at her back. Is this stark-all?
So evident the bare beyond? and only
a slender body to sustain that great bowl
which opens out above unseen? But look—
tensile, elastic, the volume of flexed thighs.

Bewildered
Anthony Howcroft

be ·wil ·dered [tr. v.]: to become lost in pathless places

'Being lost, then, is not a location; it is a transformation.
It is a failure of the mind.'
Deep Survival by Laurence Gonzales

My chance of being eaten by a shark is apparently one in eleven million.

I expect I could greatly increase that probability by moving from the indoor-heated hotel pool to swim in the sea. It's just so damned cold that I'd die of hypothermia. Which leaves cancer, cholesterol and cars as the only genuine risks and they don't fire my adrenalin. There has to be more to life than comfort, security and a steady-job. My family are thousands of miles away sleeping in a safer timezone. My cellphone is switched off. Armed with a fist of shiny foreign coins, I roam through Manhattan on this bitterly cold evening.

I'm searching for New York's underbelly, carefully avoiding anything that smells of tourists. I need adventure to distract me from a self-imposed slavery. My schedule is dictated by others, my money spent before I see it. Everything I do is laid out in safe lines and guarded by an over-protective government. There are millions like me living in your cities, fathering your children. The hours we scrape between flights and meetings are precious. They're the only things we're not forced to share. We're the permanently connected, always-on generation who secretly long to be lost.

Catching glimpses of the Chrysler building, it strikes me that she looks like a chrysalis. I wonder what she'll change into when she emerges from her concrete cocoon. Her fragile beauty is far more appealing than her taller sisters. I've drifted through the streets of many cities over the years, admiring architectures of stone and flesh. I gravitate towards cafés in bookshops, forming a literary boundary to my explorations. I let caffeine and words blur the edges until the city changes from a collection of randomly juxtaposed people and buildings into a single entity with its own character, quirks and personality. I never buy a guidebook. Far better to walk confidently and follow the surging crowds.

Instinct is my guide and I leave reason locked safely in the hotel room. There are times when the trail fades, like tonight. I could retrace my steps, but I hate doing that. Going back is an admission of failure.

Turning left I walk a little faster. This road must eventually intersect Fifth Avenue and on the corner is a gap where I'll surely see Chrysler beckoning.

No, I must have misjudged the number of blocks. I increase my pace and make more turns, walking around street corners to find something recognizable.

Eventually I have to admit I'm lost. My pulse finally begins to beat a little faster. Modern Manhattan possesses very few dubious areas so I'm not too concerned for my safety. I pass the entrance of one grand hotel where plinths contain three-foot square plots of turf, every blade pristine. They're the only green things I've seen in an hour and feel as out of place as me. On an impulse I stop to stroke one.

'It bites.'

I pull my hand back and look up.

'The city, not the grass.' she says.

My first impression is of a scam. Women this attractive don't talk to strangers on quiet streets. Not in any city I've wandered through, except perhaps those I've drifted over in daydreams.

'Thank you. I'll be careful.' I turn to leave.

'You were going the other way.'

'I was looking for…'

'Mystery?' she says, and smiles.

'Starbucks.' I say.

She slips her arm through mine she marches me down the street. You may wonder why I make no attempt to resist, after what happened to Kalpesh. That time he nearly got his head cut-off in Istanbul. He was so chained to social etiquette that he didn't make a fuss. Although I think he deliberately allowed events to unfold. He wound up in the back room of a seedy bar with a bill for 2,000 dollars and a pocket full of local currency worth the equivalent of fifty. He had a Visa card stuffed in his shoe but he wasn't going to admit that, even when they got the sword out. It was only when one of the men unzipped his trousers that Kalpesh relented.

I've never been one to go by the rules. I only appear to conform because I'm easy going. A rebel can wear a suit just as easily as a combat jacket. The woman is intriguing though, so I play her game. Tonight I've got time. Curiosity may kill the cat, but with nine lives what does he care?

We end up at an Italian bar of aluminium and white noise.
'It's got character,' she says. 'Individuality is back.'
'I like the chains. I know what to expect.'
'They're safe,' she says.
'I guess so.'
'And yet you're looking for an adventure.'
She has loose brown hair with gentle waves, the way the French do best. Her eyes are grey and impossible to read. They remind me of the crystal ball you expect to find in a gypsy's caravan, instead of the glass fakes they actually use. Her accent is hard to place, international with an American flavour. She drinks soy latte. I imagine she lives on the top level of one of those magazine-style NY apartments, open plan with wide-planked timber floors. I can picture the minimalist furniture and a row of windows supported by slanting pillars of sunlight.
'Why do you think I'm looking for an adventure?' I ask.
'Same reason we all are. Women aren't so different.'
'I'm open to most things.' I say boldly, not quite meaning it.
'Let's put that to the test.'
Pulling out a cigarette she walks towards the counter where two men and a woman are taking their drinks standing. I watch her make casual introductions and get a light. It's too noisy to hear anything more than scattered words from their conversation. She flirts with one man. I wonder if it's for real or whether they're part of the scam. I look outside. The windows reflect the interior so it's hard to make out the faces, silhouettes brushing past. I can tell that it's wet now and the light has gone underground, peeking through like stars to make the black streets glitter.
I turn to see her walking back towards our table. I wonder what she might think I'm prepared to do. Perhaps she's one of those people that like to have sex in car crashes, or maybe she's a lure for a syndicate that harvest body-parts. When I said I'm a rebel, that's with a small r.
'Drink up,' she says.
This is where I should finish things. It's easy to get out of the

trap here.

'There's a party, two blocks walk. Let's go,' she adds, confident I'll follow.
Mentally I rehearse my careful put-down words.

Before I get to use them the door to the café swings open, breaking the warm seal of this sanctuary. Without uttering a word the woman who enters instantly silences the room. Some people have a presence that can be felt like a drop in temperature. Her movement is fluid and effortless. Still cloaked by the night, her eyes flash like streetlights in the rain. Where some women are built from sharp geometries, she has no edges. Her hair is all shine, seeming to possess no colour of its own. The group at the counter move to greet her. One of the men gestures to my current companion and I realise we've not made any introductions.

'I'm Mark.' I say.

'No you're not,' she replies. 'You left him in the hotel.'

Whoever I am, I finish my drink and we leave, hurrying to catch the others. It's raining and I wish I had my coat. Each elongated raindrop feels like a thin knife. I'm exploring way beyond the limits and I know that's where the monsters live. For once though, I need to see what happens when you fall off the edge of the world.

We stand outside a block of apartments. The fire escape doesn't touch the ground and seems to go up rather than down. The sawtooth steps remind me of the raised hackles on a stray dog's back. I begin to feel claustrophobic as the tall buildings crowd around us and I wonder if they keep growing, like the teeth of a wild animal. At some signal that I miss we descend into the basement apartment. It's squeezed tight with people. The music is loud. I drink a sticky martini cocktail that's too sweet. I elect to remain sober or at least not get drunk. That's difficult though; it's comforting to sip my glass. My female companion disappears into the mass of dancers and I move away. The apartment is a labyrinth and I take yet another wrong turn. Ahead of me I see the femme fatale from the café, her hair shining with ferocity.

'It's Denis, isn't it?' she asks.

'That's right.' Since I'm no longer Mark, I decide this name will suit fine.

'Try this.' She holds out a sculptured yellow bottle and pours a cloudy liquid into my empty glass.

'What is it?'

'Illegal.'

She drinks hers like a shot. I do the same. She tops up our glasses and we repeat our actions without another word. She's exactly my height, which is six foot. My partners have always been smaller and I realise I'm used to looking down at women, physically not metaphorically. We seem very close.

Shouting erupts in the lounge. The music goes off and the silence is a shock. I turn to see what's happening. More shouting follows, but it's impossible to decipher. When I look back the woman has vanished. There are two shut doors and a corridor with a right-angle corner. I feel like Alice in Wonderland.

I look around the corner and the corridor stretches away in a straight line, ending with several steps. It looks like a fire escape back to street level. I glance towards the lounge. Two bulky men are coming towards me, blocking out the light. They're dressed in similar black outfits. It may be a uniform. I turn and run.

It's exhilarating, hurtling down the corridor. That might be the wrong word. Terrifying. The air is cool compared to the stifling heat of the party and I imagine I hear the pursuit closing. There's no time to look back. I leap up the steps in one bound. My heart hammers. A double door stands between me and the street. Big red letters on the door pronounce EXIT and I see padlocks. If this were a film I would hit the door and see it break open. Yet there's a disturbing sensation that I've been cast in the role of victim tonight. Off with his head, the Red Queen screams.

I smash into the door with my shoulder. It gives so easily that I explode into the street nearly losing my balance. I run wildly with no purpose other than to put distance between myself and everything else.

The cars are all asleep and the streets desolate. I didn't think Manhattan could get this quiet. My body goes into shock, legs and hands shaking violently. Soon I'm reduced to groping along the sidewalk like a snail. I wish I could curl back into a shell with my family. I see a black guy watching, half-hidden behind an old Lincoln. I walk over.

'Can you help me? I'm afraid I'm terribly lost.'

It helps to emphasise the English accent at times like this.

The man is hard to age. I notice he wears a silver slug curled in his ear with a single blue eye that flickers occasionally.

'Where d'ya wanna get ta?' he says, and taps the slug's eye.

I try to remember. It's a surprisingly difficult question. It seems like I knew the answer a long time ago.

'Where am I?'

'Right here,' he laughs.

'Then I guess I'm not lost.' I begin laughing and can't stop.

Jane McLaughlin

The Night Worker

I dreamed this city, its buses
with strange faces, tall red houses,
trains snaking light through dark maps.
I dreamed it when
I was in my own country, an embryo
sucking dreams through a cord.

I am one of the night people now
walking out when others sleep.
The multitudes from anywhere but here
who disappear before the real city
rises out of subways and porches..

I stand at the bus stop
with other cleaners, cooks, guards,
who never see day in winter
and think of my sleeping children.

This city dreams me
in its nightly sleep
to stand with the others at the bus stop
like notes of forgotten music
hoping to get home
before the children wake.

How to Make a Cloud

The curved stub of the cooling tower
spins grey braids, rising and twisting
through the blue air. Steam swirls and shimmers
out of its great round mouth.
The slant whorl of vapour spirals up
weaving hanks of grey and mist.
Up and up until curdling and whitening
it becomes dense, opaque.
Fluffs and bubbles at a few hundred feet,
introducing itself as a small cumulus,
joining the flock riding westwards
in a quick breeze. There's no training programme.
It does what clouds do:
looks soft and fleecy, shapeshifts gently.
Just like the ones whose perfect pedigrees
come from the schoolbook cycle
of rising mist and falling rain.

Tea

Pours a silence over
currents of talk;
green Formosa oolong.

The black shreds
open like paper waterlilies
into perfect camellia leaves
lying in a pool of gold.

A vapour of cool hillsides
wraps the sense of words.

Three blood red pictograms
two cranes and a bristly pine
on a gold sky:

I see the packet
on the shelf, and notice
a small shift in space-time.

It holds not just the green
of leaves in bright shallows
but dust blown in from the galaxy.

At the Chinese supermarket:
gold boxes stacked on trolleys.

The cranes track the star-paths.

Richard Williams

The Ending Was In the Beginning

The sun is a question mark over the horizon,
a fading of dark at the border of night.
As mercury ripples on an alchemy sea
each footstep made is further from home,
each footstep made is closer still.

Sixteen miles to circuit the island,
this metronome trance as muscles relax.
Shingle gravel stubble-grass mud,
a concreted wall to scold the tide,
the what is now and what is yet to be.

To run before six is to race the dawn,
over hardened earth and pools of ice.
A lantern moon is soon subsumed
in wan surrender under the risen light,
the spreading sweep of a somnolent sky.

David Olsen

Plumage

After too many times
through the cycle,
colour is washed away.

Garments lose their shape,
eyes surrender blue,
and the crowning

becomes inglorious
during the irreversible
autumnal drift

into ptarmigan winter.
There are no ripples
in that pool of silvered glass;

while watching that woman
daub her creams twice a day,
she sees only the furrowed

virtual image of someone
oddly reversed, not quite
a stranger. When no one

notices her passing,
she becomes invisible
even to herself.

Summer Rain

The random rhythm of summer rain
recalls a bygone year when it thrummed
on our caravan and we awoke to peer

outside, decided to forgo the primula
path along the cliff. Our books remained

untouched, a picture puzzle undone, but for
its edge and an upturned boat and nearby
hedge. You tasted of toast and marmalade

and tea, and we believed in eternity,
assumed that rain would ever precipitate

this urgent, tender bliss. We never thought
we would have to go without, that a year
of drought would deprive us of summer rain.

Patricia Helen Wooldridge

A Cup of Tea

When I check on you in the morning,
bringing your first cup of tea,

I catch you sleeping, arms flung back
against the pillow bent in childhood.

How you never sleep in your bed
after Dad dies,

but keep it made, his wardrobe full
and we never speak of love.

You always claim insomnia —
and when you wake in the middle of the night,

you like to slip your teeth back in
and that was the worst, near the end,

when your mouth was full of thrush,
sucking on ice, your gums too sore for teeth.

Coming to stay, a change from the lonely nights,
you smile, sit in the chair by the fire,

and sleep easy in this single bed.
Later, I bring you another cup of tea.

In the Museum

There have been five mass extinctions
it says on the way in.

I'm looking for the butterfly collection,
housed in tiered drawers

unnoticed, almost, this mahogany chest
in the hushed room

slide out each one—such meticulous
hand-written labels:

Ceylon, Assam, Rhodesia, Peru,

our history of theft in row upon row
of pinned thorax, indian ink,

swallowtails, fritillaries, hairstreaks,
all behind glass

with their dislodged mountings,
faded wings, jarred

from curious openings,
the silver-studded blue, missing.

Set in Amber
Lezanne Clannachan

After the storm, I walk the empty, winter beaches of Skagen in search of amber, with Torsten, a distracted step behind. As I kick over seaweed clumps, my husband creates hideous monsters which he will wrestle and tame with paper and pen once we get home. These days, since he no longer writes for publication, I like his trolls better. Created solely for our grandchildren, they have become gentler beasts, less wanton in their bloodlust.

We are about to return home, when I nudge one last tangle of mermaid-hair and there it is; a lump of golden resin like a secret heart inside the kelp.

'There's something trapped inside it,' I tell Torsten, holding the amber to the white sky. 'What do you think it is?'

Torsten squints at it. 'It's a piece of leaf.'

But I think it looks finer, like wisps of hair from a baby's head.

At home, I fix us lunch whilst he writes. Curried herring on rye bread toasted to the unbending crispness that we both favour. As we eat, I keep one hand in my pocket, twirling the amber over and over. Torsten reaches for a glass of water, his cold-tipped fingers feeling their way into a steady grip before he lifts it to his lips. He swallows the wrong way, as he often does, choking and spluttering, his fist clenching the table cloth.

'Another bone in your water, my love?' The careless humour is necessary; it stops his panic. 'That's it. Cough it out.'

His father died like that, drowned on a gulp of water. I know it's at the back of his mind, every time he reaches for a drink.

As Torsten wipes his eyes on his napkin, I sneak the amber to my lips, savouring its plastic warmth—and remember a kiss. It comes back to me as clearly as if it had been preserved in resin all these years, waiting to be chanced upon.

I forget to put the coffee on and stare out of the sitting-room window, prodding and poking at the memory to raise a little life in it. A man whose name I have forgotten, but not the salt taste of his lips. We'd been swimming, somewhere still and tropical rather than the unforgiving Atlantic that batters the Danish coast like a brat in a tantrum. He smelt sweet and warm, like raisins in the sun. I study the grey, flailing waves through the pine trees remembering the man's shoulders breaching the surface of a different sea, his skin glazed with water. Jerome was his name. The amber pebble in my cardigan pocket is silk between my age-roughened fingers. A taunt of lost youth.

'Pernille,' Torsten is saying from the hearth where he is lighting the fire. 'What about the coffee?'

The fact that he uses my full name lets me know he is upset, his low voice giving nothing away. He has always been a man of neutral tone and expression, an indication I believe, of the enormous effort it takes to keep his monsters in line. In fifty-four years of marriage, he has only once raised his voice. But neither of us were ourselves at that time. In any case, he has never needed to shout. His size does that for him. Even now, despite crooked age, he has to bow his head to enter a room; so that once he has unfolded his full height everyone experiences a small start of surprise.

'It's coming, my love. You old fellows are so impatient.'

'How can it be coming when you've been gazing out the window?'

I understand his displeasure. Coffee always follows lunch; these are the stepping stones we rely on to guide us through a Monday afternoon. Without routine, we tumble too quickly down the steepening slope of time.

We drink our coffee whilst the fire crackles like an untuned radio and a sea-wind cuffs the side of the house. This is the aural setting of my every winter's day. I shouldn't notice it, any more than I should feel the hairs on my arms growing; only now that I have, I can't sit still. I wander the room, coming to rest behind Torsten's armchair. The back of his head is puckered into three plump folds of skin where once there was a mess of blond hair. I cup the back of his head, pressing my fingers into the shallow ridges. He lifts a hand over his shoulder and we rest in that pose, our old fingers entwined. It reminds me of last summer with Hans and Lorna giggling as they buried our feet in the sand. *You're too old to hold hands,* Lorna had shrieked and Hans had dumped a bucketful of sand in my lap in a show of brotherly support.

Cocooned by the monotony of daily noise, it comes as a surprise to both of us when I say, 'I kissed a man once, you know.'

'Do you mean Jesper or Thomas, the crazy fisherman's boy?' In our first year of marriage we confessed all previous romantic encounters in the same way that you must sweep out the grate before lighting a new fire. Still, I'm surprised he remembers their names.

'Neither. It was when I was visiting my sister once,' I say, pleased at recovering another chip of memory. 'He kissed me in the Adriatic sea.'

Torsten's hand stays in mine. 'But your sister moved to Croatia two years after we got married.'

On Wednesday, Liselotte—my third and most independent child—calls to say she is coming for the weekend. She likes to escape the city with its endless carousel of cars and people. Here she is allowed to be solitary, she says. To temporarily unyoke the requisitions of friendship; all that collective eating, dancing, fun-making. *It sounds like bliss*, I always tell her and she laughs and complains it's tiring. In those moments, I see how truly young she is; careless with her perceived abundance of time.

After the phone-call, I find myself staring into the back bedroom and the lifetime of discarded furniture blocking any light from the window. For a moment, the weight of that unwanted collection sits on my chest and I struggle to breathe. That's when the idea comes to me.

'I want Liselotte to stay in the back room,' I tell Torsten and watch his face closely. 'Everything in there must be thrown out and the walls need re-painting.'

Torsten looks at his watch.

'The bus to Vesterby leaves in ten minutes,' he says. 'I'll need some paint.'

Of course he doesn't ask why we must use that particular room; he is made of that old, patriarchal stock, trusting his personal interpretation of the world above the deflecting notions of others. Then he adds, 'You're pacing, 'Nilla.'

I stop marching about the kitchen and put my coat on.

On the bus I worry about which colour I will choose. It has to be powerful enough to bring life to a room that has never been used before; a room that has been weighing down our home like a dead limb.

Torsten has only just started emptying the room when I return. In the hallway, lies a roll of carpet and six upturned chairs, legs in the air like cartoon sheep struck by lightning. He remains on the far side and we have to talk across the junk.

'You haven't made much headway, have you, my old man?'

'I've been busy enough.'

I prise the lid off a tin of paint, tipping it gently forward, to show him the colour. 'This is cheerful, isn't it?'

'It's an honest blue,' he says, nodding. 'Like the colour of a baby's eyes.'

And for a moment I panic, glaring at the paint and worrying that yet again I have chosen the wrong colour.

When we first moved in, still wearing our nuptial gleam like winning medals, my mother wanted to know why I needed a house with four bedrooms.

To fill with babies, I told her.

Then she questioned my choice of room for the nursery.

Why this small, dark one at the back of the house?

That was my mother; always trying to tweeze out the sinister motive behind everyone's actions.

I told her my daughter must feel safe. In those days, before scans and such, we relied on sixth sense, the body's voice, and I knew I was carrying a girl. I told my mother the baby wouldn't be used to space and light after nine months in my belly. I must ease her gently into this world. The room was going to be quiet, womb-like and I would paint it a dusky pink for warmth and softness.

As soon as the paint dried, I realised I'd made an awful mistake. The pink had a faded and dusted-ridden quality, like something existing only in memory. Early one morning, whilst Torsten swam in the sea, I passed my baby girl onto the nursery floor in a drowsy puddle of blood. An other-worldly being, curled in on herself like a translucent snail. Her head rested in my palm, so thin and malleable, I was afraid it would take on the shape of my cupped fingers.

That day Torsten raised his voice at me.

How could you lose our baby? He'd screamed. *How could you be so careless?*

As though I'd misplaced her, set her down like a bag in a coffee shop and walked away, humming.

After lunch, when I go to stack the kindling in the hearth, I notice there is something wrong with the firewood. It has the planed surfaces and paintwork of something that belongs indoors and like a puzzle I try to piece it back together. The colour keeps poking me in the eye until I realise it is the same marmalade orange as the bed we inherited from my grandfather; a present on our wedding day. I leave Torsten to struggle down onto his knees with the matches, only to find an empty hearth.

The sight that greets me at our bedroom door, forces a string of curses from my lips and I am furious with my inability to absorb events in considered silence. Our room is huge, dizzying with the unimpeded flow of air. All that remains of our bed is a dark rectangle on the floor where the sun's scuffing light had, until now, been unable to reach.

'You've chopped our bed up,' I shout over my shoulder. 'What will Liselotte think when she comes on Friday?'

'She will assume we are two old people going a little crazy.' That's what he says.

I join him back in the sitting-room and watch as he makes a fire out of our bed's splintered remains. I conjure up that kiss, let me tell you. A kiss such as I'd never before or since experienced; a lesson in perfect contradiction, violating and seducing both. I understand now it was little to do with the man in the surf and everything to do with my wish to inflict damage.

'I'm not making coffee today,' I say.

'Then I shall make some.' Torsten rises from the hearth, drawing up his full height with much dignity despite the audible bone-cracks.

'You don't know how.'

'I didn't know how to chop up a bed this morning,' he says. 'But I managed.'

He returns with coffee, precariously balanced on the board I use to cut raw meat. He has failed to find the tray and apparently we shall drink our coffee from water tumblers this afternoon.

'Why did you hack our bed to pieces?' The glass of coffee scalds me with gathered heat.

'Because we have to start over. Nothing is the same.'

'It was just a...' I can barely say the word now that I'm on it. It requires the lips to soften and part under its formation as though just saying the word betrays the speaker's desires. 'Kiss.'

Torsten shakes his head, staring hard at me. 'It was a door to an alternative future.'

That night we paint furiously side by side. We manage a single wall and it looks to me like a cresting wave ready to sweep away all those visceral-pink memories. Then we lay out roll-up mattresses and sleeping bags from the garage and make a camp at the foot of the blue wall. Torsten lets me zip the two bags together so we can hold hands before we sleep. Our bedtime ritual has survived his axe.

Sleep steals Torsten's fingers from mine and I am left awake in a room quiet as held breath. Then he shifts and coughs deep in his throat, like he's clearing a water-bone. He is not sleeping; instead he has been mulling over something he wants to say.

'There was a girl once,' he says, his voice disturbing the room's peace like a hand tearing cobwebs. 'Her name was Nana.'

'Nana? Nana Pedersen, the wife of your best friend?'

'Of course not.'

'Nana what's-her-name from Oveby who had that bicycle accident?'

'No.'

'Not that Nana who looked after the chickens on Nick's farm?'

'I don't know any chicken-lady.'

'Then who?'

'A student from Copenhagen. She came for the summer.'

At regular intermissions throughout the night, like the slow rotation of a lighthouse beam, another question lights up before me in the darkness. He sleeps between his answers.

'Why would some city girl want to write a thesis on your foul, old goblins and how come I didn't meet her?'

Torsten's eyebrows are freckled with blue paint as he turns to look at me. 'You were at your sister's.'

In sweeps the blue-glass of the Croatian sea with Jerome, bellydown on his surf board of polished wood, hands out to snatch me up like a fish. He was a friend of my sister's husband, a Dutchman on holiday. And there I was, also alone, with an empty ache in my belly.

'I wasn't gone for long.'

'But you were, 'Nilla. The whole summer.'

It wasn't how he'd pictured the summer to come. The rocking chair he had painted and brought onto the verandah so his wife and newborn baby could enjoy the warm evening breeze, creaked alone. He put it away in the back room, avoiding the dark stain in the middle of the floor. Then came a knock on the door.

Nana, it seems was drawn to all things oversized. *Human beings are small on the outside but huge on the inside*, said this wise, little thing from Copenhagen. Her thesis explored the dark brotherhood between trolls and our own psyche. She quoted Ibsen and wore inappropriate shoes for this part of Denmark.

'She was always tottering, on the verge of falling over,' says Torsten as we walk off paint fumes on a frost-hardened beach. 'Always in need of a steadying arm.'

'A tree to snake herself about,' I offer.

And yet, for all my husband's corporeal sturdiness, it was his chimp-limbed, bulb-eyed, boulder-headed beasts she was most taken with.

'But there were looks,' he tells me. Moments that arrived in sudden silence and caught them both out. Those sweet, unexplored possibilities. The same ones I tasted in the surf on Jerome's lips.

Liselotte comments on how ridiculous the new IKEA bed looks in our old bedroom. Still, she's quite happy to sleep in it for a few days. She laughs, shaking her head, when she sees our campbeds in the back room. She is truly Torsten's daughter, asking no questions for fear of the unwanted intimacy they might attract. When she's gone, we retrieve the hatcheted remains of our marital bed from the garage and continue to burn it.

'You are right,' I say. 'A kiss is not just a kiss.'

Torsten nods at the fire. 'And we are all trolls on the inside.'

When the snow thaws, I put the amber bead into my coat pocket and take Torsten on a long walk, deep into the empty flats of marshland behind our home.

'Pernille,' he rumbles. 'We're getting lost.'

But he is wrong. It has been some years now since I last took this path, but every step is sown into my feet. When we reach the cupped hand of earth, hidden from the endless horizon, he peers over its edge.

'There's nothing down there,' he says, frowning at the knee-high bramble.

'You must be brave,' I say and unnerve him with a kiss. He steps forward to steady me, as my feet catch and trip on the matted gorse, and together we descend into the earthy hollow.

'What an eerie place,' Torsten says, glancing around as I rip the vegetation aside. 'A troll-hole if ever there was one.'

'That's where you are mistaken.' I straighten, so he too, can see the small cross, nothing more than a pair of sticks twined together, standing guard over a knot of hardened earth.

'You see, I didn't lose her.' I press the amber into the small mound under the cross. 'I knew where she was all along.'

Rosalind Hudis

Erosion

A year since we last climbed this path
to where the field's sentence
falls, unfinished, to a speechless glaze.
Sea; a single boat hovers
like a pause-mark. Already edges
are closer, there's less of anything
that stands for firm. Cliffs glister
into air as if addicted
to an ease of giving
themselves away.

Balanced here, ruins of Monachty'r Graig
behind us, we could be something
salt-air has whittled, so porous
time could funnel through.
And it seems effortless to be this,
almost generous. The farm
eating itself from the inside, half-gone,
not empty, but spacious, loosening out
through a breach in the roof
where sky leans in.

Heart Patch

For him to sew a patch
across the tiny abyss
in your four month heart,

the surgeon
must have you chilled,
your breath postponed

in a pause
outside the beat
you were set to.

As you slip
below the heat-line,
an arctic incubus

wells up through
your skin. We run
at the speed of death

down corridors
rimed with day-break
while nurses course alongside

like snow-geese migrating,
unstoppable and urgent
as they press you

between thermals of wool.
When the wind lifts you
out of my arms to theirs

I remember this is the day
of solar eclipse.
The moon will defer the sun,

muffle its pulse,
draw night's simulacrum
through the lunch-hour

of junior physicians
while they settle off-time wings
on the courtyard benches.

Their sandwich foil
that unmeshes the sun
into fractions of a rose window,

will smoke over,
like a moment known
to all the work-force of hearts

in partial eclipse.
Later I'll forget
even to remember this,

subtracted from the daylight,
in a waiting room
on the rim of your theatre,

I'll think of the surgeon's hands,
dough pale and trimmed,
between butcher's and tailor's.

Maria Grech Ganado

Platinum
for my sister

This early morning, quicksilver in my mouth, I
sketch you closer, as a midsummer bird, or some
Byzantine Emperor, somersaulting like a clown.

Wake up wake up—you are so precious still
upon this heap of dust and leaden hearts.
For you I will unravel with my tongue those
webs our dying father tangled in his last trance

returning you to bulrushes in Egypt and reeds
of songs our mother sang distracted, rocking
our wawa in the treetops close to the sky—
their music haunts me yet, mysterious, sprightly
as light, teasing my soul with flickers
like beeswax in the night…

Aisling Tempany

On being alone
after the painting by Frances Richards

There I am, a crudely drawn figure
in oil, on a piece of board
outside the main exhibition.
A glass frame encloses me,
surrounds me and confines me,
with the lines of a bed and a table.
The only company in my small place.
I have no expression at all.

The Sewing Class

This is their language—needle and thread.
All their words are in a trouser leg.
Their verbs are satin, cotton and taffeta.
The pronouns are voile, chiffon or organza.
The dress Samira wears, auto-didactic,
lets her speak in hues of green of her children,
the hem translating her marriage.

Question

You say to me
'how are you'
and I tell you.
I tell you how I am upset;
I tell you how I am excited;
I tell you nothing,
trying to smile and
breaking into tears.

You say to me
'how are you'
and I tell you.

It never occurs to me
that you're not asking
a question,
that you're just being polite.

David Batten

Beyond the KT Boundary

a lizard flows over stone
like a fish shadow
on a barren sea floor
sickle-shaped hole in light
a hawk warning

creatures of the margins
salamanders that survived
the fires that passed over
that birds gazed down upon
wrecked dinosaurs
greened the planet
and summoned me
to bask on my tile
my piece of mantle
to stare up into blue nothing
where the galaxies weave
new mysteries new outcomes
stories I could never believe

Colonist

I let the drought-wind scrub my face
slick my hair back until I became a figurehead
cleaving a sea of pressures

while tree roots were fingering
down through soil silently searching in the dark
on the iron scent of water lengthening
strengthening blind filigrees of the tree's behest

the tree and I leaned in opposite directions
one almost flying about to take off from the face
of the earth: the other deepening ties

flung birds took notes
flowers turned their heads following other directions
the sun burned its attention on everything

A Fractured Self
Eithne Nightingale

Germaine stands with her back against the window, placing a hand on her right hip. Joshua goes down on one knee and points his camera upwards at her naked torso streaked with light from the half open Venetian blinds.

'Left foot forward,' her urges. 'Turn your body to the light.'

Then he moves in on her face, lowers his camera and zooms in on her upturned breasts, decapitating her. Unexpected clouds screen the midday sun, casting a film over his muse and for one moment the light is perfect. He quivers, a pleasure so intense, and presses the shutter tight.

He repositions the camera. Refocuses. A strutting elbow. A hand cupped around a handsome hip. He motions to her and she turns around as clouds regroup. The light is fading. He does not have much time. He readjusts the frame to capture her tattoo, a snake charmer on her shoulder seducing a cobra rising from the small of her back. Then the light slides off her buttocks and skims a pair of ankles with tendons as slender but firm as the stem of an amaryllis lily. She anticipates him and lowers her body onto the floor, easing herself into position, her tangled, auburn hair weaving outwards across the floor boards.

'Stay there. That's perfect.'

Germaine keeps her eyes tight shut as he stands over her, shooting from every angle. Outside the rain is gentle at first. Soothing, reassuring. Then it hardens, gathers strength and hail hits and bounces against the ground. She shudders as a door bangs shut.

'Keep still,' he shouts.

She opens her eyes and freezes. Joshua is towering above her, focusing on her unruly bush. He opens the aperture wide; maximizes the depth of field trying to get the exposure right. But there is barely enough light. He twiddles the dials. Backwards, forwards. Then he presses the shutter tight at the exact moment the lightning streaks across his subject.

'Brilliant. Wonderful.'

As Germaine dresses and prepares to leave, Joshua slips her a ten pound note and takes down her address.

'I will send you an invitation. You must come to the private view.'

She is not to feel shy or embarrassed. The photographs will be beautiful but anonymous. No one will know she is the model and he will not disclose her identity unless she agrees. There will be nothing disrespectful. It is art not pornography.

Several months pass before Germaine receives an invitation to the exhibition, *A Fractured Self,* illustrated with a black and white detail of her snake-charmer tattoo. At first she is reluctant to accept the invitation. She doesn't mix in artistic circles. She was keen on photography when she was at school, but she has not had much time for anything since the birth of her daughter, Emma. Now her social circle is confined to the mums and toddlers group on the North Peckham estate. In any case, she only agreed to do the shoot for the money. Not that she earned that much. Ten pounds for what turned out to be a whole day was far below the minimum rate. It was a neighbour, who always insisted she was the best looking woman in Peckham, who had recommended her to Joshua. No, she will give the private view a miss.

But the cobra seems to encourage her. Perhaps it would be interesting to see the photographs after all. She will think about it. As the day approaches Germaine plucks up the courage to ask one of her neighbours to look after her daughter. She will go for half an hour and take a peek at the photographs incognito.

Clutching the invitation, Germaine makes her way to a converted warehouse on the edge of the River Thames. She has tied back her auburn hair as she knows that will be a tell tale sign. But when she walks in the place is teeming and she cannot see the images. People dressed in sombre black are talking ten to the dozen in posh accents and sipping champagne. She wishes she had dressed in something else besides her pink top and white jeans, but her wardrobe was limited.

The speeches start and the guests move to the far end of the gallery. At last Germaine can see the photographs. She stands back from the large black and white prints, which cover the fifteen foot high walls at almost treble her height. The first image shows her tousled hair waving outwards across the floor boards. The second, her slender, alabaster ankles. The crowd is clapping. The first speech is over. She moves onto the third image. A decapitated torso, the light from the half open Venetian blinds falling across her breasts. She moves onto the fourth. Toes as large as a row of huddled baboons. And to the fifth. Buttocks the size of an elephant and, centre stage, the unruly thicket of dense bush, the intimate details of every single hair captured and bathed in an extraordinary light from when Joshua pressed the shutter at the exact moment that the lightning struck.

Germaine shudders and tries to compose herself. And then she realizes the significance of the red dots under the images. She tries to add it all up in her head. Over sixty thousand pounds and the night is not over yet. She remembers the ten pound note Joshua gave her after the photo shoot and thinks of all the things she cannot afford, the rent overdue, the bills not paid.

The speeches end and Germaine and the crowd circulates. She can no longer view the images uninterrupted.

'Wonderful depth of field, just like Edward Weston,' says a young man behind her, 'And brilliant use of light.'

'All that penetration,' says his companion, an older man by several years, examining every detail of her pubic hair. 'Weston screwed all of his models after the shoot, you know.'

'Lucky him. Nice bit of skirt… That is, without the skirt,' sniggers the younger man.

Germaine withdraws, stumbling over people's feet and knocking over glasses. She refuses all offers of champagne. She has not come to hear people make insinuations about her. How dare they? What has Joshua said about her? She looks round to find him. He is in the centre of the room, moving with ease amongst his guests; revelling in the limelight and responding to the questions of attentive journalists.

Fired by the cobra sliding up her back, Germaine approaches Joshua and taps him on the shoulder. He turns around, disconcerted to be stopped in full flow.

'Ah. You have come… I am so pleased.'

'I need some air,' she breathes. 'I need some air.'

He excuses himself from his guests and steers Germaine away through the crowds, out of the warehouse and along the quayside. The hazy light of the veiled moon ripples across the water towards them and a drizzle hangs heavy in the air. Barges, tethered to the quay with snake like coils, bounce and butt against each other.

Joshua slips his camera over his left shoulder and his right arm around Germaine's waist. He slides his hand over the cheeks of his muse's firm buttocks recalling every view, every angle through his long lens. He shudders with pleasure as he remembers pressing the shutter tight just as the lightning struck. It had been difficult to restrain himself, but there was no reason to curb his desires any further. Besides his friends assumed he had made love with Germaine. They expected it of him. Best not to disappoint.

Joshua leads Germaine down moss-coated steps to a barge below. Ignoring the whirlpools of empty beer cans and disused milk cartons swirling around at their feet he holds out his hand to help Germaine into the boat. But the muse reaches into her bag and takes out a small spray canister. Germaine has used it once before on the estate when someone threatened to steal her benefit and she is glad of that experience now. She lifts the canister as if to take his photograph and presses down with her thumb, filling the air between them with a billowy spray of burning mist.

'You've blinded me, you bitch,' Joshua cries as the pepper reaches his eyes.

He falls backwards into the Thames, his camera flying through the air and hitting the water with a loud thud. Germaine smiles, her 'fractured self' restored.

Chris Considine

Mother's Last Christmas

Not the last of her life but the last
when she could cope with freedom,
an unfamiliar room.

We drove over the moor in a blizzard,
held our breath on the dips and rises,
the old house a longed-for refuge.

No neighbours, no lights from distant farms,
no birdcalls, even the snow fell
in a windless silence

and froze silently. There was
no going out on Christmas Day
to the plain brown chapel

where if there were no kings
there would be shepherds,
and three girls playing brass instruments —

mother and I confined to our stone shelter,
our fire, tête-à-tête meals
and radio. No visits

no visitors. Every morning I trudged
the half-mile to the sharp steep curve
gleaming with untouched ice

and every evening at the open door
described to my blind listener
the silver moon, the unreachable silver hills.

Marcus Smith

Wonder

The painted trees I love to paint
Bore me more than an old book,
And I am full before I even look,
A thin, tired glutton worn away
By restless roaming. Visiting now
Is a question to explore, my agitator,
My gruff stranger demanding,
'Is there more?' I must direct
This troublemaker—and gaunt ghost—
To amazement's nearest door,
The superbly crooked river walk
Under dancing, dawning hills
I no longer find enthrals.

Travelling on, and sick of travel
And hungry for more than wonder,
I sometimes wish wonder would end.
I envy prisoners and the blind
And long for a wonderful prison,
Longing only to stay a short time.

Pilgrimage to a Desert

I lie in the cold night, shivering.
I still have thoughts and feeling.

Wind scrapes against sand.
Sand scrapes against land.

A bird cries above the scraping.
Cries scrape away horizon.

My organs begin to groan
Louder, longer than they've have

Groaned before. Tell me the thing
I came to the desert to hear.

Fugue with Her Ancestors

A wax carver from Russia, he rode a horse
    (She likes to watch a candle burn, burn down)
All the way to Hamburg and married a circus rider
    (But pities the one-track lives of trick horses)
Whose son left for England and ended there as
    (Blinkered as greyhounds chasing a metal hare)
A bookie, card-sharp and dog-racer
    (Her father inventing pills in America)
While she wonders why not travel elsewhere
    (And spent his end tallying great, great sums)
While she most fears becoming somebody
    (In his dirty bathrobe, every day the same) like the next
While she changes her wardrobe as often as she can.

Gabriel Griffin

Domo to Geneva

Rain all along the lines and lakes from
Arona to Domodossola. Then sluttish snow
began to slur the windows, a white dust trample
shoe-stains in the corridor. The train whirred through
the black hole of the Simplon, our Janus faces
a series of slides tear-streaked, finger-printed, smudged

as is my memory of you. You liked
Switzerland, the ordered life, no surprises, the cows
slaughtered in whistle-clean abattoirs, out of
screaming, out of sight. Not Italy, no, Italy with its
haphazard landscapes, hooting cities, its history and
art and myth a Macedonian salad — Italy wasn't for you.

You told me once in Rome you'd visited Keat's
grave; a nameless headstone heaped just the same
with flowers: purple iris, yellow roses out of season,
lilies, violets in the February grass. Behind weeping
trees an incongruous pyramid. 'A pyramid!' you'd
exclaimed, 'Under such English rain!'

Uneasy all the time, unsure, you'd check
the name at every station and still stop
the conductor each time he passed. Our windows
whipped through stations hard with iron, cement,
those waiting ignored the silver lines that
carried us away. I wept.

What's certain? Not your death — I wasn't there. They said —
but what have words to do with you? For me, you're still
travelling on that train, a TGV, the one that rushes past
the one I'm in, hurtling up-line; so fast I can't see you
looking out, perhaps for me, white face against glass. Snow
falls thick and slow, the tracks ahead are black with ice.

The Singing Fish
Melanie Whipman

I bought the singing fish from a travelling salesman. A species I'd imagined as extinct as the rag and bone man. My mother used to talk of them, tapping at the door with miracle cures for the ailing housewife. When I was little I imagined some strange hybrid—a Magic-Male-Avon-Lady, doffing his hat, with a white-toothed grin and cheap charm, with eyes that slid past my mother's face to the darkness of the room beyond. She invited them in sometimes, she said, for a cuppa. I wanted to ask if she used Dad's mug, or the china cups we kept for best, with the blue bridge and the birds. I struggled to see her with another man, pouring out tea at the kitchen table, perhaps laughing, with that fluttering gesture she had, of touching her nose with the back of her wrist. She was never the type to chat to other men—she was a mother, her accessories were aprons and oven gloves, her perfume was TCP and chicken stew. I tried to picture her—would she sit, or stand? At opposite ends, or closer, across a corner, like she did with dad, so when they cradled their cups, their fingers would touch, across the formica. Like Ed and I used to do. Chloe loved the cups too, she liked the pictures—a scene frozen in time, lovers on a bridge, and swallows scissoring a china sky.

My travelling salesman came on Tuesday morning. I'd been sitting at the window since sunrise, watching the darkness leach away and the houses opposite creep back into focus. You could tell it was going to be another scorcher. I closed my eyes, stretched myself out across the open frame, waited for the flick of air against my face, perhaps the cool weight of a shadow, the tap of fingers, the scent of summer skin. But the air was soupy-still, no slip of breeze to shift the smells around, and in any case, the flowers are shrivelled now and the verges are like rectangles of tobacco. I can still smell the river though. You can't see it from here, but you know it's there. They say its hit a record low this year, the water turgid, the banks carved and cracked. Impossible to imagine its winter force, they say.

Ed had gone to work, hours before, his goodbye-breath warm on my shoulder as I stood at the window. The children in the street trailed past, in puffs of dust, shouting and shoving, skipping and yacking, with caps and plaits and red faces. The milkman had been and gone long ago, the two litres of semi, the granary and the bacon were tucked in the fridge. I'd left the front door open, on account of the heat, so he must have knocked on the door jamb, or perhaps he leaned in, and used the knocker. I still polish it. It's Chloe's height, she used to laugh at her reflection, all fat faced and foreign. I look like a fish, she used to say, gupping her mouth up and down in silent song. The milkman didn't shout. You'd have thought he would have called out. A cooee, or a hello. Out of courtesy. I'm a good customer; I've tried everything in his little brochure. I was in the loo, at the back, but I would have heard him. It's behind the kitchen still. The neighbours have had theirs moved. But I like it there. I grew up in this house, it seems disloyal to change it, and in any case it was handy for toilet-training. And Ed used to leave the door open when he came home from the factory. He'd tell me stuff about his day while he showered, his voice slipping out with the steam, as I stood at the stove making supper. We used to talk about having an en-suite put in, for Chloe. She'd already chosen the sign for the door, this kitsch silhouette of an old-fashioned tub bath, with a little girl, head and shoulders safely above the waterline. If the milkman had knocked I would have had a chat, on the step, just the usual. Hot enough for you? Who'd have thought it could have lasted this long? The usual litany of pleasantries. Small talk's under rated.

But the milkman was long gone when the figure appeared at the top of the street, a pencil sketch, scribbled on the skyline, gaining colour and definition as he came nearer. He was heading straight here. Past Vera and Barb and Mrs Coney at number thirty-three. My heart was in my mouth, he approached with such purpose. Then he stopped, and I could see the case he was carrying, and I started breathing again. No one official would deliver news with a box like that—some huge square, black thing, like my dad's old projector box, the one we used to watch the slides on at Christmas. Or a magician's box. It made me think of the time Ed and I took Chloe to France, on Brittany Ferries, the overnighter. We let her stay up to see the magician. Amazing Mike. There were people without kids and Ed was laughing, in the way he used to, in silence, with his eyes watering, and his cheeks puffed out, and his chin dipping down towards his chest, as if he were embarrassed about letting it out. He kept asking what the heck they were doing there, without kids? He's a practical man, and it was a shocker. But Chloe loved it. She liked all the tinsel and glitz, and the little shimmering frock his assistant wore. Until he made her disappear. She was only gone five minutes, but Chloe got all worked up. She yanked her thumb out of her mouth and shoved herself off my lap, head swivelling, hands pleating the bottom of her dress. It was the blue and white striped one I got from the French catalogue; it's still in her wardrobe on the padded pink hanger Mum bought: My Favourite Dress. I thought she was going to howl, but then the woman burst out of some cupboard on the other side of the stage. Fanfare. New outfit. Good as new. And Chloe's all smiles.

The salesman wasn't just stopping to re-adjust his grip on the box, or wipe the sweat from his face, he was talking to Mrs Gibson's cat. I took the opportunity to stretch a bit, change position. I was kneeling on the seat Ed had made me, with the special squishy cushion, so my legs don't go to sleep. I shoved the heel of my palm against the sash and leaned out. He was bending down, beginning to stretch his hand towards the cat. It's a vicious old ginger tom. It had a crack at Chloe once, sent a ladder spinning up her tights. Not that she was fazed, she just came running home and grabbed a tin of John West out of the cupboard. It took a while, but she didn't give up, she kept tuna in her bag for weeks, and she finally won him over.

I was holding my breath, waiting to see what the cat was going to do. Perhaps it was that squat, black box, or the stillness of the morning, or the fug of sulphur in the air, that was turning the factory smoke a grubby yellow, like an old bruise that's getting better. Whatever the reason, my heart was juddering, and I was expecting something special. From here he looked like one of Chloe's Pelham puppets as he hunkered down, folding and concertinaering in on himself. He reached his hand out, slow and gentle, and then I saw the sudden spasm of his body as he snatched himself back, jerking away, his arms windmilling as he toppled over onto the pavement on his backside. It was as if some giant hand had slashed his strings. His yell reached me a nanosecond later.

I laughed, a strange huff of a sound that came up from my stomach to my throat, and the back of my hand was against my mouth, and I caught my reflection in the side window, and it looked like my mother.

I was still smiling when he knocked at the door. He stood there in his liquorice suit, a polite pace away from the threshold. 'Morning Maam.' Like an American cowboy.

'How's your hand?'

'You saw that?'

I nodded and, when he held out his hand, knuckles up, I took it in mine. It was a nice hand, tanned, flesh-levelled nails. Clean— he didn't work in the factory. There was a row of raised welts across his skin, oozing blood and fluid.

'Come inside. I'll get some cream.'

He followed me, past the Z-bed in the hall, into the kitchen. The first aid stuff is in an old shortbread tin under the sink. It caught me unawares for a second and I was glad my back was turned to him when I prised off the lid and looked inside.

'I've got all sorts here.' My voice was fine.

'Really, it's not necessary.'

I put it on the kitchen table in front of him. 'Antiseptic cream? Bites, stings and grazes. Or maybe Calomine.'

'You've got the lot.'

Calpol, Tellytubby plasters, teething gel, Infacol.

'Piriton—that's best. And it's still in date.' I gave him a proper spoon, the plastic one didn't seem right.

'This'll work, will it? Stop the reaction?'

'Should do. Might take a while—it's nasty, and you'll have scars.'

The lid was a bit gritty, where it hadn't been used for so long, but he got it open, and it was fine inside. He didn't say anything, just tipped it slowly into the well of the spoon. I looked away when he put it into his mouth.

'It'll make it better—ease the reaction; the itching, and swelling.'

He was filling up the spoon again.

'Tea?' I put the kettle on, dithered for a second, over the Willow Pattern or the mugs. It's a small kitchen, and I had to step over his box to get to the larder. 'What made you come here?' Close-up the box was even bigger.

'I sell stuff.'

'But why here? To this house? You came straight here.'

'Did I?'

'Yes. Sugar?'

'Just milk. Should I sit down?'

'Sure.'

He didn't move, he was waiting for me to indicate a chair.

'Just sit...' And that's when I realised he knew. I saw his expression. He was afraid he'd sit in the wrong place. In Chloe's place.

'So why did you come?' I wasn't angry, most people know anyway. It's an old story. He took the seat opposite the fridge. I could see him out of the corner of my eye as I filled the teapot. He was staring at the photos. The fridge door is plastered with them. All stuck on with a magnetic alphabet. It's partly how I taught Chloe to spell. As she got older we used to write messages to each other with them.

PE tomorrow.

get marmite.

packed lunch Fri

Luv u

'I see you at the window.'

'Oh.' I sat next to him and poured out the tea.

'This is a short cut for me. To the office.' He cradled his drink with his damaged hand. 'Well, garage really. With a desk. I sell stuff on Ebay.' He kept his eyes on the cup-people on the bridge. 'I do all hours. Early mornings. Late nights. Have you seen me? Red Fiat. With a taped wing mirror.'

'That's you, is it?'

'I just catch this glimpse, of your face, at the window. Always there. Whatever time I pass.'

He was just a boy really. Eighteen, nineteen. A couple of years older than Chloe would be now.

He peered over the rim of the cup. 'I wanted to ask. I mean, it's been bugging me. Are you there, at night too?'

'Sometimes.'

Often. The city's beautiful then, the sky folds in soft as a whisper, and sometimes you get the edge of the sunset, seeping across, bright as fire opal. Like the picture Chloe did at school, where you do a wash of colour, and then sketch on the skyline afterwards, with charcoal. She put in the river, curving round the town in a series of S's. Her sky was much too bright. Mango. When she brought it home from school I held my hands in front of my eyes, put my sunglasses on, pretended to be dazzled. I wished I'd hugged her, said it was perfect.

'You stay there all night?'

'Sometimes. Sometimes I sleep in the hall, on the camp bed.'

'One of your neighbours bid on something. Collection only. I asked about you.'

The picture's upstairs on her bedroom wall. The mango's faded now, more dusky peach.

'She said it was a car accident. Your parents and daughter.'

'On the bridge. No one's fault. Ice. Mum and Dad dead.'

'Your daughter?'

'They've not found her yet.'

His eyes slipped away from mine and he turned his gaze to the bridge on the cup. 'Heard melodies are sweet, but those unheard are sweeter.'

I shouldn't have let him in. He could be a psychopath. Or one of those weirdos who tell me they can 'reach beyond the grave'.

'It's Keats.'

'Oh. The poet?' So he's one of those. You'd be surprised how many people do that when they know. Mostly its prayers or passages out of the bible. Occasionally a poem. Sometimes one of those corny little American books full of homilies. They used to drop them through the letterbox, or give them to Ed to pass on to me, as if my grief gave them some new authority. Not that I minded, there's nothing left to mind about. I wait for him to elaborate, to start chucking out wisdom.

'Keats—he's writing about the scene on an urn. How time is frozen in art, how it'll stay like that forever, I guess. He died young.'

'It was five years ago.'

'And you think she might still be alive? Might come home?' He shunted his chair back, bent down and began unstrapping the leather bands on his box.

'She used to swim there in the summer. In the river.'

I'd wait with a towel, and she'd come out beaded with water, her hair in sopping rat-tails and her body cool and solid against mine. Her skin still smelling of her, beneath that brackish river smell.

'So you're always waiting?'

'Yes, in case… Supposing she came back and I wasn't here. It's possible, she swam like a fish. She got badges. I sewed them onto her costume. So many, we ran out of space. I put the rest on her bag.'

He nodded, earnest, eyes serious. He was a nice boy, Chloe would have liked him.

He delved in his bag. 'I've got an idea. I've got something, I think...'

'Other children were nervous of swimming in the river, but not Chloe.'

He was rummaging inside, practically up to his armpits. Mary Poppins.

'How about this? D'you reckon it would help?'

He pulled it out. Fish have always looked prehistoric to me, gaping and sliding in the shadows, like they're searching for a past world.

'It's a bass. It talks. It's got a sensor. Kind of an alarm. With a message. Hang on a sec, I'll switch it on. Now wave your hands in front of it. That's it.'

It was a huge rubber thing, green and gold and strangely muscular. I humoured him; moved my arms, like windscreen wipers, and it leapt into motion, flicking it's tale, turning its head, grinning inanely at me as it began to sing: 'Don't worry. Be happy.'

'Jesus!'

'Mad, isn't it?' He was grinning too, and for a moment he looked like a fish himself with his wide mouth and his wet round eyes.

He was a bit 'odd.' But there's nothing wrong with odd. I nodded slowly and held out my hands, 'Chloe would have loved it.'

This morning I am all prepared. I put the fish in the alcove, by the door, on the telephone table. I adjust angles and heights, and finally it sits waiting in the shadows on top of the Yellow Pages. It is all ready to go - customised by my strange salesman, so I can put in my own tape. I imagine Chloe and my parents watching as I test it out. I think they'd like it.

Ed comes home, slow-stepped and seamed with black. He triggers it off as he walks into the hall. It flaps its tale and opens its mouth,

'Hello Chloe, if it's you, then welcome home darling...'

Ed flinches and stops. I see something swirl and flicker in his eyes, then he shutters his face and shuffles silently into the kitchen. I don't know what I expected. He locks the bathroom and showers for a long time. When he comes out he lowers himself into the chair opposite me and forks in his bacon and egg. 'This is nice, love.'

Later I sit on the window seat and he sits in his arm chair, and we watch the news together. There seem to be people dying all over the world. At 10.30 he levers himself up, presses his lips to my hair. 'Good night.'

I follow him into the hall. The fish is waiting with its watery welcome, batteries charged, voice ready.

'I'm coming with you.'

He stops, his body still twisted in retreat, shoulders hunched.

I lay my palm against his cheek. 'Let's go to bed.'

His face folds up and his mouth opens, and he makes this noise that comes from somewhere deep in his stomach. When I hold him, I remember the shape of his body, and the way we used to fit together.

Kaddy Benyon

Milk Fever

You, my Eskimo mother—those
low-slung cheeks, watery eyes hidden
inside a fur-lined hood, breasts you
couldn't unpack in time for your milk

to be supped unfrozen. You strapped
me to a sled, wrapped tight in pelts,
a matted fleece, some buckskin
stretched and dried that summer

I grew inside you. There was a reek
of hunt and meat; of a thick blood
pulsing the air with each numb
thud of your boots kicking up ice,

spangling my hair. North you trekked,
the sled ropes tied to your waist
as you grunted, sweat and chapped.
All I wanted was for you to stop,

hold me in sight a moment, not leave
me tethered to a lumber pole while
you hacked pale blue blocks, stacked
them to build a snow-dome shelter.

You lit a fire in its pit, heated meltwater
in a wide, silver bowl and held it
steaming wildly to my lips. Head dipped,
you left me in a darkness of sniffing

bear and fox, padded beyond earshot,
were lost. Waking under drifts of white
linen, I hear breathing beside me
and roll over to touch you, nose-to-nose.

Amongst Women

This time I will not miss you. I will not
miss you because I will not think

about you, your turquoise sweater, mother
of pearl buttons at your neck. I will not

look for you in a crowd or wish for you
to call. I will not dream I am your daughter,

your postulant, your friend. I will not pray
for you or to you, *Blessed art thou*—

No, this time I will barely notice
that you are gone, gone. This time.

In Vitro Heuresis

If we lived in ancient Athens
we might celebrate the mystery

of our purposeful design. You,
me, consciously conceived

that I may live, love, survive.
Beneath a shedding moon

you reaped the lonely cell of me,
transferred me temporarily

to the temple of your mind—
the blood music beats, the earth

root retreats - where we incubate
in liquid darkness, syncopate

our disparate tides, monitor
each doubling and sluggish

doubling, the uncoupling
of my halves. You are my secret,

surrogate other nursing a soul
at dawn, each nub and ridge

and bump of me bit-by-bit becoming
a kicking little homunculus

front-crawling to the lip
of a petri-dish world to emerge

noisy, hungry, woman, whole.

Noel Williams

Under the Bridge

It was not the last day I rode that bike:
my hands tacked to plastic, bell big as an apple,
the sun oozing over the embankment
to make toffee of the tarmac.

Not the last day of summer I'd scoot under my bridge
where the road tipped into darkness;
plough the red wheels up the roadside dump of gravel,
wheels drowning, shovelling, stuck.

It was not the last day wild grit
sprayed up to my knees, as I heard
tractors joust beyond the embankment,
rooks spar and flap with the racket of parents.

It was the day I understood *now* slides
in tiny stones. Coming home
to no radio by the sink, her empty coat hook,
Dad gripping the puncture kit with meticulous fury.

Domestic News

On a lighter note, Horatio
the hedgehog trapped in a well
in Steeple Aston, Oxfordshire for seven days
appears to have gnawed the likeness of Christ
in the Ryvita his rescuers lowered yesterday
as this (enhanced) photo clearly shows.

Meteorologists predict the snowfall
in our living room will subside
before the week is out. Debate on global
warming continues in the kitchen. Hall meltwater
no longer threatens the hat-stand. The cat
has moved upstairs.

Sometimes you huddle close,
the colour of my stories flickering on your throat.
Sometimes you stretch away and crochet
in the wastelands of the distant cushions,
barbarous garments falling from your fingers.
I report the day as I see it, not as it is.

Finally, our main stories again.
Horatio, it turns out, is Henrietta.
The exchange rate in the bedroom
continues to fall. Analysts predict
the coldest summer for years.
The sun, they say, will burn out to dead rock
well within our lifetime.

Talisman

This is about stone. Stone is time:
Clifstán. Stánrocc. Old words almost eroded.

On the balcony of grandma's doll's house
in the cobwebs of our garage I laid stones of childhood:

milestones, stepping stones, way stones.
One from Bournemouth, bright with sea-wet.

One the whorl of ammonite cracked
where the creature had bloomed into air.

Soft gems of tar. The dead stare of marble.
Gritstone muted by the greys of moss.

All those stones are ground now.
But here's one I've pocketed. It's a landscape

my thumb can interrogate.
You laid it in my hand from the tilth of our first garden,

dug with our fingers, sticks, a seaside spade:
red as a pulse, ticking under scudding light,

as if fallen from an alien sky,
as if, *stánincel,* little pebble, heart-stone,
time would be stalled whilst I held it.

Charlie Darling
MWS

Charlie Darling was cleaning the windows when I arrived. I didn't take much notice, the Estate Agent told me about a local handyman who did bits and pieces around the house; I was useless at all that stuff, so left him to it, pretty sure he'd find me when his money was due. I had moved back to Newport. I didn't need such a big house, but I was told it made sense. 'Even if you *don't* expect to be in Newport for more than a few years, you should maximise your investment.' So, there I was, twenty-eight, single, and 'maximising my investment' in a City I thought I'd left forever.

'He'd work for nothing, you know, if money is a bit tight.' A man was leaning on the five bar gate. 'He loves this place, been working here on and off as long as I can remember; I should know, I've been on the lane over thirty years, myself.' He'd pointed at Charlie, but it was me he was sizing up, wondering how someone so young—I could have easily passed for twenty-two—was able to afford a place in *his* world. I was surprised he didn't call me *son* and ask for my parents.

'I haven't even spoken to him yet,' I said, 'I'll be at work a lot, anyhow, and money isn't a problem, so he can just get on with it.' I enjoyed saying the last bit and purposely didn't offer my name—then again neither did he—I wasn't intending to join the Neighbourhood Watch and I guess he wasn't about to invite me to his Bridge club.

'Charlie comes with the house, pretty much,' he said, 'doesn't say a lot, good old chap though.' I was offered an offhand wave and my neighbour carried on up the lane.

Charlie was sitting on the patio table sucking on the remains of a rollie when I came in from work. He looked up and nodded as I sat opposite. I offered him a Marlboro; he made a slight shake of the head and continued to suck the dregs from his damp cigarette. We sat silently, just smoking. He was scanning the garden and I took the opportunity to sneak a look at him. He was a bit shorter than my five ten, with a grey Bobby Charlton comb-over—which should have been comical, but wasn't—and a weathered, mud-coloured face that was difficult to age, but I guessed at mid sixties; he wore an old pair of paint spattered overalls, which smelled of fresh tobacco and newly picked potatoes. Charlie caught me looking. I blushed. He casually held my gaze for a moment and tilted his head, dragging my eyes to a space by the patio doors. The blank wall I left that morning was now home to a freshly painted wooden frame covered in lush Clematis.

'It looks great,' I said, 'what's the damage?' I pulled out my wallet, glad for an excuse to cover my embarrassment.

'Just scrap; moved the plant from behind the trees, like, no good there.' He flicked his dog-end into a freshly dug flowerbed, nodded again, an invitation to follow him, and we walked the grounds. 'I'll build a new rockery there,' Charlie nodded to a pile of stones collected from the garden's many flowerbeds and rockeries: he did a lot of communicating with nods. We carried on walking. 'Want a vegetable plot?' his eyes did the pointing this time, to a dried circle of grass, probably collateral damage from a kid's trampoline.

'I don't have much time to cook vegetables, Charlie,' I said, 'I'm working most of the time.'

'I can do that.' He almost smiled, 'and eat some if you like.'

Probably exhausted by all the talking, Charlie nodded again and walked out of the garden.

We shared many sparse conversations and silent smokes over the coming weeks. I often worked late, but whatever time I came back, Charlie was there, either working the garden or sitting and smoking at the patio table. I didn't see much of him at weekends in the first few months, as I would get up late and go for a run or play tennis with some work colleagues, but as time moved on I found myself spending more and more time in the garden, inexpertly pottering about, moving rocks or barrows of earth from one end of the garden to the other. I was nervous to begin with, nervous that I may upset Charlie of the careful equilibrium he created, but as it became obvious that he was happy with my amateur interventions, I began to feel more comfortable and became more adventurous. He started to give me tasks and projects, nothing too big, manageable jobs suited to my limited experience, but I launched into them like an eager child allowed up late to help Dad.

'A water feature'd be nice, like,' Charlie said as he passed me a rollie, 'big job, mind, not cheap.'

'What were you thinking, something like an angel pissing in a pond?' I sniggered at my joke. 'Or a big fuck-off dragon spewing water instead of fire?'

Charlie produced his nearly smile. I was getting attached to that look, not *really* a smile, but whatever it was, it made me feel like a member of some exclusive club. 'Never seen a pissing angel, like,' he said, 'but was driving the other day and seen this dragon fountain with spread-out wings in a garden-centre down St Melons.'

'Been window-shopping, have we, mate?'

'No! Just passing-by, and thought I'd mention it, like, no matter.' Charlie looked away, sucked the life out of his rollie—wasting at least three good drags—and crushed it under his heel. He started to get up.

I jumped in quickly before I lost him. 'Reckon we should get it, then, mate?' I asked.

Charlie sat back down, almost smiled at his feet and began to retie an already right shoelace. 'You're the boss,' he said.

'But you're the brains,' I replied.

The tennis took a back seat and I didn't feel like running anymore, I was getting plenty of exercise digging and lugging things around the garden. Work had been the most important thing in my life and, since leaving university, everything had rotated around it. Edinburgh gave me a first class degree, good mates and a loyal, attractive girlfriend, but I left them all behind, just as I had left Newport four years earlier. I landed a well-paid job in the City and started my life again. Work was all I had really thought about for the last six years. Now, for the first time, it was becoming a chore, something to do just for money rather than satisfaction or enjoyment, something in the way of life, not its purpose.

We hired a flat-back truck to collect the dragon. The lads at the garden centre were surprised that we intended to take it home. These things were normally delivered to councils or country houses, but with their help we safely roped it to the back of the truck. I was wearing a dirty t-shirt, camouflage shorts and a pair of builder's boots, my skin brown from working in the sun and my hair hidden under a Toronto Blue Jays baseball cap. Charlie was in old overalls as usual, a lined face always ready to be nodded or tilted, but the top of his freckled head was hidden by the twin of my cap. We could have been workmates collecting materials for some important client or a father and son helping each other on some family project. I smiled inside and jumped up beside Charlie. 'Home James.'

'Yessir.' Charlie tugged the tip of his cap and started the chugging diesel engine, 'your wish is my command.'

The dragon wouldn't have looked out of place in a park or a country estate. It took us all day just to stand it upright in the garden, then nearly four weeks of evenings and weekends to get the fountain working. The house sat in a plot of more than an acre, yet he towered over it from every angle.

'What do you think of my idea now, mate?' I asked. Charlie and I were sitting at the patio table looking up at our working and smoking, as usual.

'Your idea?'

'Well, you may have played a little part in it,' I said, grinning at Charlie's blank expression. 'So, what do you think?'

'It's just right, like, just right,' he said, 'I'm glad *you* thought of it.'

We rearranged the rest of the garden around the dragon, moving plants digging up flowerbeds, creating new rockeries, aligning everything to focus on our new centrepiece. I invested in a professional lighting system so that even in the dark he could keep an eye on the house. I kept my curtains open at night; the dragon was the last thing I saw before I went to sleep and when I woke up in the morning he was there looking at me.

Charlie was working on a 'Welsh flag' flowerbed and I was preparing the bedding plants at his side. 'Is this garden grand enough, mate?' I asked, looking at our work. 'This dragon bit is amazing. But don't you think the rest is just... well... *too normal?*'

'We do the best we can,' he replied.

'Yeah, but what if he doesn't like it? What if he would prefer to be somewhere more exciting, somewhere grander than our boring house-garden in Newport?'

'It's only a stone dragon, like,' Charlie said, 'and nobody can have everything they want.' Charlie's expression didn't agree with his words.

We no longer sat at the patio table; it had been broken-down with the other garden furniture and rebuilt as a spectacular wooden nest—a flash of genius from Charlie. We just couldn't wait to source the proper materials, so we cannibalised everything and anything we could find, but hadn't got round to replacing them. Unfortunately this did nothing for the garden's identity problem: the more spectacular the dragon looked, the drabber the rest of the garden became. We still sat and smoked most evenings, but on chairs dragged from the kitchen and I was only smoking rollies now; it felt better to share with Charlie, especially as I was spending most of my money in garden centres and builders merchants.

I spun my eyes around the garden. I noticed flagging tomato plants. So much had changed since Charlie first offered to create that vegetable plot.

'I never had a garden when I was growing up, Charlie,' I said, 'I lived with my Nan, half way up a block of flats in Alway. I sometimes planted things in the window box, but they usually died. I did grow some great cannabis plants in my teens though. Nan thought they were tomatoes and kept asking me when they would be ready to eat.' I chuckled and looked across at Charlie, expecting to find a raised eyebrow.

'Everyone does that in Alway,' he said, without any change of expression, then held up his cigarette, 'but these days I'm happy enough with this.'

Charlie's wife came round one Sunday morning, after he had slept over for a couple of nights. I didn't know he was married. We spent a lot of time together, but neither of us talked much and it never occurred to ask abut his family. Charlie was just... Charlie.

'When you coming home, Charlie?' She looked a lot younger than him. If I *had* thought about him being married, it wouldn't have been to a well-spoken, attractive, middle-aged woman.

'Been busy, love,' Charlie stopped digging, but kept hold of his spade. 'I told you on the phone.'

'I know that, Charlie, but you didn't say *when* you were coming home? Angherad came round with the girls; they were upset when you weren't there.' Charlie's wide didn't appear surprised by his absence, just wanted to find out when she was likely to have him back. I looked on, didn't say a word; didn't feel it was my place and if I spoke to her she would become more real. She was already realer than I felt comfortable.

'I'll see them next time; tell them… yeah, I'll see them next time.' Charlie kissed his wife on the cheek and continued to dig. She smiled at me, I nearly smiled back and she left, leaving us alone with out work.

My Boss had another word about my 'uncharacteristically shoddy work and lack of effort.' He was also concerned about my appearance. 'You're a good looking man and usually so smart, but lately…' Getting rid of the dirt from under my fingernails was difficult and I always had more important things to do than iron. I went to the GP and got my first ever sick-note; a month or so in the garden would sort things out.

The dragon looked magnificent, but we were still puzzling over our next project. Charlie thought he would look better still if separated from the rest of the garden, so we created a moat around 'Dragon Island'. We were pleased when the moat was complete, but soon wanted more and it swelled to a pond, which grew into something nearer a lake that overtook the read of the house.

There was an old conservatory on the back that didn't get much use; we decided to knock it down and build a bridge from the backdoor to Dragon Island. Charlie and I were pulling it apart when the 'delegation' arrived: six of them, said they represented 'The Lane.' Charlie and I were sitting on our kitchen chairs, at the edge of the lake, sharing a rollie.

'We did knock,' the spokesmen said—it was smug, 'lived here more than thirty years,' man—looking uncomfortable in his new Marks and Spencer casuals, 'but we didn't get an answer, knew you were here so…'

'Yes, we heard you,' I said, 'but we're busy,' I proudly raised my arms and gestured towards the garden, 'as you can see.'

'Well, yes… well that's the thing we are concerned about, you know, what you are doing with the house.' He was trying to keep his eyes on us in defiance, but couldn't stop them straying around the garden and up at Dragon Island. The dragon's head could be seen from outside the house, but the rest of him was hidden and the full impact of what we had achieved could only be fully appreciated from within its midst.

'Do you like it?' I asked.

'It's not a matter of like, is it?' he gasped, 'look... look at the size of it, all this water, this can't be right. What about the foundations?' He suddenly realised what else we were doing. 'And that beautiful old conservatory, no... Alice and Edward spent hours in there, they loved it...' His voiced trailed off as he also registered the trench we had dug, designed to channel even more water around the garden.

'Yes, it was a nice conservatory, wasn't it,' I said, 'but we needed the space for a bridge.'

'This has always been such a nice neighbourhood, I... I... Charlie?' He looked past me, pleading. 'Charlie?'

'Yes?' Charlie lit another rollie.

'Charlie... I... What?'

Charlie shrugged and took a long drag on his fresh cigarette.

'Sorry to be rude,' I said, 'but we have to get on, the conservatory won't pull itself down, will it? You can let yourself out.' We stood up and grabbed our tools. The disgruntled neighbours mumbled 'well I never' and 'who do they think they are,' then huffed out as one. 'You haven't heard the last of this,' someone called back as they stomped through the muddy hallway.

It didn't take too long to complete the rest of the project, we worked every day and late into the evening. The porch in front of the garden came down too and we built a bridge from one end of the front door to the five bar gate. Much of the garden was now under water; in fact the entire garden was one big lake other than a few tree islands, a path around the edge and, of course, Dragon, perched on his nest, wings unfurled, breathing liquid fire into his watery world.

I went back to work when my third sick note ran out, sporting my navy pinstripe suit, a crisp white shirt with a red silk tie and ten freshly scrubbed fingernails. I had been off for twelve weeks it total. The MD was very kind; until my 'little problem' I had been shaping up as his top Director, targets exceeded and budgets under strict control. He said he was glad to have me back on board; I told him I was pleased to be back and was feeling much better.

I scanned the office, remembering for the first time my many awards and achievements, now decorating the designer walls. I looked through the glass partition to a bank of analysts busily clunking away at their computers. Six years and three promotions ago, I was one of those analysts clunking away in a similar office in London. Now I was back in the place of my birth working in a brand new office and the youngest Regional Director in the company. I looked back at my plush desk, piled high with files, sitting next to a computer invisibly storing many, many more. I whistled a long sigh.

'He *is* beautiful Charlie,' I said, passing him a rollie, 'I suppose I should say handsome, but beautiful suits him better.'
'Yeah, beautiful.'
As the sun set, we sat, smoked and drunk milky tea. I was fidgeting and smoking more than usual. It was Sunday evening, I was working in the morning and needed to catch up; I stayed late at the office every day and then put in even more hours at home. Charlie still found things to do around the house, as well as keeping Dragon Island in shape and looking after the fish we had introduced to the lake, but we had finished our major project and I could no longer get excited by planting a few flowers or trimming hedges on the weekend.
'Do you think he looks a bit lonely up there, Charlie?' I asked.
'Yeah, maybe a *bit* lonely,' Charlie replied, looking up and taking unusually quick drags on his rollie.
'Perhaps it's like Guinea pigs, mate; you shouldn't keep them on their own, you know, they need to live in pairs.' I was dreamily making small talk, not expecting a reply, used to talking around Charlie and receiving a lazy response every few sentences. I didn't have to wait long for a reply this time; as soon as I had finished Charlie jumped in.
'I've seen another one, not as beautiful as him, like, but sort of pretty, you know, and spouts really fine water that if you put a red light on it looks like proper fire. It was in a catalogue and even bigger, only a darker colour, like, it's in England somewhere, over the bridge and...' Charlie abruptly stopped talking.
This was the longest sentence I'd ever heard him speak and I could see he was struggling to hold himself back. 'And... And... Come on Charlie?'
'Just saying, that's all.' He looked away, puffing hard on his rollie.
'Just saying what? You can't fucking say "just saying, that's all" and then not say anything.' I was almost shouting. I never shouted

at Charlie. 'Do you think we should get it? Is that it? Come on Charlie. Jesus! Say something.'

'Don't know.' Charlie was struggling to regain his usual calm.

'Charlie! You brought it up; you can't make the longest speech of your life then clam up.' I was shaking.

'It'll be dear,' Charlie said, pointing his rollie at Dragon, 'even more than him, I reckon.'

'Okay it'll be expensive, but apart from that, you think we should get it, then, yeah? Do you, Charlie?' I couldn't stop a broad smile stretching my face and Charlie was failing to close down his first ever grin. 'So?'

'You're the boss,' Charlie said.

'But you're the brains,' I replied.

Alex Josephy

Fukushima, Mile End

Two in the morning, bolt upright in bed, I left behind your calm breathing, left you the London night, another room. Two five. Mouth dry. Things I said today. Things I didn't say. The clock flashed, green *phosphorus*. All my foolish life. Two ten, eleven. Spectacles? Lost; looked beyond. Through. Walls *starting to melt*. The window, panes all fled. I saw the house opposite, long and low; *the stricken reactor*. A crane flew over, fell; the grass stirred. Singed. But wait. *Helicopter* crop circle, lenses open wide. Two eleven thirteen, sirens; beneath the wailing, fizz and spark. *Containers breaching*, one two three, two eleven thirty. How I wished. What's gone, what's promised, forgot. The clock-face red, a zigzag trail. The sky *spiked* orange. Clouds roiling. Everything ruined, wrong. Walked out onto the earth's rind; skin a kettle, feet boiled dry. Two eleven fifty; how much *in one second*? *Rods merged*, sinking. Concrete. Rock. Fire-ladder down, down through the bowels. Saw the fifty workers walk in, walk out, take in turns. *The peril*. Two twelve. Men in yellow spacesuits, rounded limbs like babies, faces hidden, carried water. What else could they do?

A New Beach

No-one saw this coming,
invading the waves with its weave
of particles, veil over veil thrown down

at the water's edge,

a hushed crescent
where yesterday the tide
rattled in over rock and grit.

They're shaking their heads
in the Post Office. It's known,

such things come to no good,
these sands that glisten,
tricks of the ocean.

Already there are shells,

a dropped ribbon of weed,
two oyster-catchers
picking out a zigzag track

on stiff twig feet

and somewhere up the coast, a whole village
is waking to the drag and moan
of undertow.

Rosie Garland

Dark Matter

The night sky over Darfur overwhelms
with stars. It is so burdened, there are plans to cull
a quarter. A third. More. They will prune back
the constellations to their chief brightnesses—
the named, the mapped—burn off the stubble
of the small, the feeble, the unclear.
Torch the unimportant to cinders.

They will dam the Milky Way, divert
its flow to those who appreciate fine light;
leaving the star-field uncluttered
for the Lords of the Blackness:
Antares, Altair, Arcturus; extending
ashy vacancies between these oases
in the night's new desert.

Drinking the Water of the Nile

I leave my clothes to the neighbours.
Dresses of local cotton gaudy
with leopards, shirts creased at the elbow
from leaning across the desk. They can't understand
why I am leaving so much behind.

What are you going to wear?
I lie; say my mother has sewn a new outfit
to welcome me home. I try to clean the floor.
Although I get down on my knees
I can't get rid of the grime of cockroaches.

I scrub my teeth with gritty Libyan toothpaste, raise
a final glass to rinse my mouth. Fatma tattoos
my fingertips with henna. It looks
as though I've dipped them in blood. She gives
me a tiny basket so tightly plaited it can hold water.

At the railway station I ask about the journey
to Khartoum. The ticket collector shrugs, clicks
his tongue. *Three days. Maybe five? If God wills it.*
As the train slumps northwards, firecrackers rattle
the evening, celebrating Eid. A sheep's throat is cut.

Nicola Warwick

Accidental

Sometimes, I find messages in strange places;
a marble, a shell, a white feather in a pocket
where I know I haven't left them. And sometimes
I see trails from aircraft scratched across the sky,
lines of scribble, stretched around the speckles
of a galaxy. Now and then, I find my hand
grasps a pen and sets it free across a page,
firing off a stream of words that might make sense
in another context. Maybe all this is the conversation
with myself I'd rather not have, like asking
a question of someone whose answer I already know,
yet hoping this time I might be wrong.

Homunculus

I have your voice
but not your means
of expression, not your power,
not in any way
that favours possession.

I sit in your mind
swaddled and gagged by your thoughts,
your actions, entirely forewarned
of your mistakes.

And I know how things
are set in motion, how
the tick of an action
echoes on
once it has stopped.

I know these things;
your missed chances,
your failings
and unawares.

I know you as more
than your skin, your desires,
your needs, can predict
your next move, sense
the kick of each synapse.

I know you in more ways
than you know yourself.
I know all this.
I have your voice
but I cannot speak.

The Reticulated Man

By the time we meet, he's already dressed
in his suit of reptile skin, so, as always
I swoon over the cut of his scales,
how they overlap to a watertight sheath.

Down his back, he sports a tiger's black
and gold, his belly pale as a vampire
and I'm caught on two fronts. He folds me
in his coils and his face is faultless,

no lines, no smiles, no expression.
I know I'm one in a line of prey
that he's caught and wrapped for the taking.
I know I'll be squeezed and taken whole

as he wraps me round and round,
binds me tight as a mummy, coercing me
to silence. This time, I'll come willing and charmed
by his movement, the smooth definition of profile,

beguilement of his eyes. He will leave
just my fur and feathers on the path behind him.
I know one day he'll forget himself
and shrug off that coat of cold-blooded calm.

I'll watch, crushed and stifled
as he splits open his hide and walks free.

Jericho
Vivian Hassan-Lambert

Etta May Josephs opened her eyes wide as the whistle blew. She'd been sitting in the same clothes for two days and her mouth was dry and sour. She leaned back to look out the window at miles of farmland, which stretched out in every direction. She had always loved the sound of trains. As a young child, when she'd heard it chugging and blowing across the fields of Georgia, she felt it was calling to her. Sometimes she would run to the crossing and watch as the train sliced through countryside, a brown monster with flaring nostrils and a trail of steam.

In the three and a half weeks since Etta had left California, she'd only spoken to her nephew and her father twice—once from the general store and a second time from a neighbour's, paying the cost plus a few cents extra. It had been exciting, like in the old days when people didn't have telephones of their own. Jeffrey, the boy she'd raised since the age of three, told her news about school and she told them both about Grandma Kaye's funeral, about the house bursting at the seams, the flowers, the food, the singing and the weeping.

The railway carriage was practically empty. A white man and small boy sat at the far end. The boy wore shorts, his knees were scraped and he swung his little white legs, tapping his heels against the seat. His father, in an ironed striped shirt, looked out the window and handed the boy sandwiches neatly wrapped in waxed paper. The boy had light brown hair and mischievous looking eyes and reminded Etta of the child she looked after back in L.A.

The train lurched around a sharp bend as another train passed in the opposite direction. Etta strained to see into the passing train's windows as it moved in a blur of metal and glass.

A lady in her early thirties now took the seat across the aisle. She had on pale white stockings and a small felt hat, the sort women used to wear to church when Etta was a child. Hardly any folks used trains anymore, now everyone was flying with those fancy stewardesses, or driving cars, and Etta didn't care much for either. The train swerved then whooshed into darkness. The wheels hit metal tracks and filled the carriage with screeching, then, as it whipped back into light, the steady pulse of wheels on sleepers returned like a lullaby.

Etta had spent the night in her seat. She'd taken off her shoes, put a net over her hair and pulled the crocheted blanket she'd taken from Grandma Kaye's over her shoulders. She woke a few times as the train pulled into small country stations. In the morning she felt achy and tired; she brushed her teeth and washed her face in the tiny bathroom, then went to the restaurant car and ate fried eggs and ham for breakfast. Now, with a satisfied stomach she sat enjoying the scenery as it passed, letting her mind go to other things.

She thought of her Cousin Wendell. How close they had felt at the funeral, as if their childhood were only days in the past instead of years. His stutter was worse, yet he was still gentle and sweet, and he seemed to bring warmth into any room he entered. He had helped with the preparations—writing a note for the local paper; talking with the Reverend; fixing the screen door; collecting plates and dishes from the neighbours. And on the day of the funeral, and the gathering afterwards, he had made it feel as if Grandma Kaye was there watching over them, filling all their hearts with strength and longing.

The ticket collector entered, a white man this time, which seemed unusual, with his ticket machine strapped diagonally across his chest. When Papa James had worked the trains, travelling between Detroit and Chicago several times a week, he'd worn a white uniform with buttons as bright as melting butter, and though he still had to say *yassuh* like some old plantation boy, he was happy enough with the job, when thousands of others were lining up at soup kitchens across the country. Even now, his meagre pension helped to pay the rent on their house in Compton.

The ticket collector was at the far end, punching the man's and boy's tickets. He was chatting, making the boy smile, teasing him about something, using his arms and hands like an airplane. He pushed his pill-box hat forward so that it looked as if it might fall and this made the boy laugh harder. Out the window Etta could see cattle grazing—brown ones for beef, black and white for milk and cheese. She thought of Br'er Fox—the stories Grandma Kaye used to tell—how he'd outwitted the Cow and got all her milk. It made her smile to think of Grandma, wrinkling up her old brown face and using her fingers like claws, trying to scare the children who sat listening at her feet—and sad to think of Grandma Kaye, born nine years after the war, the keeper of stories, now dead among the willows.

Etta's hand went automatically to the brooch which sat just above her breasts. The brooch was pale brown and ivory and though Etta had only recently started wearing it she felt it had become a part of her, like her eyes or mouth. It looked pleasing against her even brown skin and it felt warm from the sun coming through the window.

The ticket collector had finished with the man and boy and was swaying down the aisle towards Etta and the church lady. 'Tickets,' he shouted. Etta snapped open her pocket-book and brought out the ticket: neatly folded, pink with bold blue writing. The ticket collector stopped between Etta and the church lady then turned with his back to Etta.

His trousers were too big. A chain hung in a loop from under his jacket; it was connected to a punch which he was now using on Church Lady's ticket.

'Mam,' he said to the lady with a slight bow when he was finished, then he turned to Etta.

She hadn't seen his face clearly before. He was older than he looked from afar, maybe in his mid-forties. She held up the ticket, but he didn't take it, so she dropped her hand obediently down in her lap and waited. He was chewing gum, breathing hard between chews, flicking through a little pad of paper and making marks with a pencil which he kept stored behind his ear. Even over the rhythm of the train, she could hear the breath between his nostrils, puffing like a horse or a dragon. His face was unshaven and there were deep tired creases outlining his cheeks and mouth. He leaned against her seat—forming a wall between Etta and the church lady—a little closer than she felt was proper. She moved back to accommodate him.

'Ticket,' he said, keeping his eyes focused on his little pad of paper.

Immediately Etta recognized the tone; she had heard it a hundred times before, a million—travelling to school on the bus in Detroit; at the Science Museum in Los Angeles; on an outing with Jeffrey; and now here, on this decrepit train—it made the hairs on the back of her neck rise like a troop of invisible soldiers. In resignation, she raised her hand and the ticket collector snatched the ticket and stared at it for a long time, swaying back and forth on his heels, considering. He looked at her, then at the ticket, shook his head like something was wrong, let out a wheeze of air, then shook his head again—it felt like minutes passed.

'Problem?' said Etta, feeling herself grow hot and impatient.

The man wasn't going to answer; it was like he was waiting for something, trying to make up his mind, and the lady across the aisle, with her blue pocket-book and her hands folded neatly on her lap, was staring straight ahead.

'Bet you got some good home cooking in there,' said the man finally, pointing his chin in the direction of a basket that was on the seat beside Etta. It was full of wool and cotton which she had found in a chest at Grandma Kaye's, too good to waste.

'Well,' said Etta, ignoring his question. 'Is there a problem?'

'Might be,' said the man, snapping the ticket in his fingers then sliding it into his gapping jacket pocket.

Etta felt a surge of alarm; the pocket was shallow and she could see her ticket, just within reach, its pink tip protruding like a tiny folded handkerchief. She had to stop herself from leaping forward and grabbing it, her heart racing and her stockings cutting uncomfortably into her thighs.

'I asked you about that basket,' he said.

'I heard you.' She slumped into her seat, trying to ignore him.

They passed a group of farm buildings and Etta pushed herself to think of all those women singing at the funeral. They'd lifted her spirits, even in her grief, and she'd felt washed by their songs. Now she concentrated on keeping every muscle of her face from moving, not wanting to give him anything, no sign of fear, irritation or despair.

'I asked you a question,' he said again, 'and it ain't polite not to answer when you're spoken to.'

'I heard you.'

He looked down at his pad, then back at her. He had one front tooth missing and his uniform was creased and threadbare at the edges. They were passing miles of brown flat fields now—occasional trees, bare of leaves, thin grey skeletons against a giant sky. She thought about storming out of the carriage or grabbing the ticket out of his pocket—but he was bigger than her, and he probably wouldn't even let her stand. It was the kind of thing he was used to, putting women down, coloured women in particular.

'Travelling on your own?' He said, tapping his fingers on the rough upholstery.

She closed her eyes for a moment and tried to summon up those songs.

Jericho, they'd sung.

Joshua fought the battle of Jericho.

'This ticket is from Savannah,' said the man, interrupting the beat of her silent song.

'I've paid all the way up to Los Angeles.' She could feel his eyes travelling all over her, pinning her down.

'You don't smell like no movie star now, do you?'

She tried to ignore him, keeping her eyes focused on the seat in front, its red leather head rest curling slightly at the edges.

'That's a nigger city, Los Angeles, ain't it?' He looked over his shoulder for a moment to check who was listening, but the church lady looked straight ahead as if the man hadn't spoken, and the boy and his father had disappeared, probably to the restaurant car.

'It was better when people knew their place. A car for the coloureds, a car for the whites, drinking fountains separate.' He bent towards Etta and lowered his voice to a whisper. 'You might even think the same, an attractive nigger lady like yourself; travelling all alone as you are.'

She could feel the touch of his damp breath against her ear and in a sudden rush of heat, every pore filled with sweat, then fingers of cold spread across her back, like a dead person pulling at her from the grave. His watery eyes moved from her face towards the folds of fabric on her chest and her hand went automatically towards the brooch.

'Wowa,' he said. 'What have we got here? Steal it?'

She wanted to lash out at him like a wild animal, to push him down, to scratch and bite, to grab his throat in her hands, but she kept herself still, waiting and ready, the way she had been taught by her father and Grandma Kaye.

Then she felt the touch of his finger on her arm, pressing at her, sending a shiver through her spine. A low stupid animal-like moan escaped from her throat.

'Flesh and blood,' he poked. 'Flesh and blood, steal it?'

She looked desperately across the aisle for some kind of acknowledgement, but the church lady kept her eyes focused on a spot towards the end of the carriage, as if she were in a different train than Etta, going in a different direction.

The train rushed forwards and all at once Etta felt a stirring inside—a sudden shift and cracking. She closed her eyes and her head fell back against the seat. She took a deep breath.

Jericho, Jericho

Her grandmother's spirit took off, rocketing through the sky, bursting into clouds, breaking into thunder—angry and astonishing.

Jericho, Jericho

She took a breath again, opened her eyes and looked towards him.

'Take your hand off me.' Each word spilled from her lips, quiet and forceful.

The man pulled away, but she felt the pressure of his finger still lingering on her like something she could never get rid of.

Then the man spoke again, timidly first but quickly rising. 'I blame that King nigger myself,' he said. 'Marching and protesting, gets everyone agitated. Ain't natural.' He looked towards Church Lady, but she showed no sign of listening.

Etta thought of King's beautiful serious face, how Jeffrey had gone to hear him at Wrigley Stadium, about his word-of-God preaching and his tone of fiery hope. She thought of how King had turned the other cheek, how he'd been hit without hitting back and she looked at the collector, summoning every ounce of strength, wanting to frighten him with the power of stillness.

'You swallow those words,' she said. 'You're not good enough to lick at the soles of his feet.'

Etta's face was covered in sweat; her heart was pumping in her throat. She looked straight into his eyes and something in the man seemed to crumble. The train collector moved backwards. He opened his mouth then closed it like a gasping fish. He looked tall and off balance—a building about to topple. Suddenly, he bent forward, narrowing his eyes and coming so close Etta could smell his acrid breath. But she was strong now; she could feel it in her bones.

'Sassy bitch,' he said. 'Sassy nigger bitch.' Then he pulled away, stood up and tugged at the ends of his jacket.

He had said it now, what he'd been longing to say all along, and at once Etta could see him as a boy—striped t-shirt, sling shot, chipped tooth and a wad of gum—a bully even then. She grabbed at the arm of her chair and squeezed.

'You best get my ticket and punch it, now.'

They passed a train yard and the train called out a series of short whistles.

'My ticket,' she ordered. 'Punch it.'

Slowly, and without looking directly at her, the man took the ticket out of his pocket, held it for a time, then pulled the metal punch from a chain on his belt. He hesitated for a moment then let the punch fall to his side without using it. He rested his hand on the edge of her seat.

'Things have changed,' she said. 'And you better get used to it.'

After the defeated man finally punched the ticket, he rushed to get out of the carriage, grasping on to the backs of seats as if he might fall.

If she ever saw that man again, she would—

'Well, I never,' interrupted the church lady, just as Etta was thinking about getting up and stretching her legs. 'He can't treat people like that,'—and when Etta didn't answer the lady continued—'he just can't'.

Etta turned.

The woman was so pale and thin, she looked like a rattling china cup about to break.

'Well, he did,' said Etta, arms folded across her chest. In an hour they'd be out of Texas and into Arizona. She thought of sixteen-year-old Jeffrey—he would never have let the ticket man talk that way. But then Jeffrey would probably have ended up in jail with a bruised eye and busted ribs.

'It's against the law,' continued the woman.

Speaking rude to a coloured woman? Being a coward and a bully? Ignoring her?

The train plunged into darkness, the wall-lights flickered and went out.

'I admire that King,' the woman's voice persisted. 'He's terribly handsome, and a lovely voice, your people must be so proud. He and Kennedy were friends you know. Sad when Kennedy got shot, I just cried and cried. Who could do a thing like that, kill a president?'

They were in the light again, flying through tiny stations where rickety huts had stood for decades. How strange that now the man was gone, this woman couldn't stop herself from talking.

She could see that the woman felt nervous with her fragile hands fidgeting in her lap.

'Oswald,' said Etta.

'Pardon?' said the woman.

'You asked who could do a thing like that. Kill a president.'

'Oh,' the woman giggled. 'I know, *Oswald*.' Then the woman erupted into cackles of high-pitched laughter—so surprisingly free and out of character, it made Etta laugh too. Somehow, now, despite all that silence and fear, she felt connected to this little woman, with the screeching laugh, who hadn't lifted a finger in all that time when she could easily have done so.

'So, you going to Los Angeles?' the woman said when their laughter died and they had rode awhile in silence. 'I'd love to go—the Grauman's Chinese, Hollywood Bowl. o you just adore it?'

Adore it? thought Etta. They had the little house in Compton with its front yard and back, the Church on 116th, Jeffrey's school, her job at the Langhams.

'It's where I live,' she said.

But the woman didn't seem to hear, she was off in her own world, rattling on about Elizabeth Taylor, Doris Day and Jimmy Stewart. The boy and man, who had been gone quite some time, came back into the carriage laden with an armful of soda and chips.

'By the way,' said the woman after the boy and man had settled into their seats, and her own talking had slowed to a bearable pitch, 'what *do* you have in that basket? Is it something to eat?'

A sly thought wormed its way into Etta's brain, something foreign and sickly, good enough for nightmares. She thought of Grandma Kaye—her gnarled hands knitting to the end—of Jeffrey and his talk of revolution—and for some reason, she couldn't say why, she didn't feel like telling this tiny woman the truth of what lay beneath the basket's lid.

'Hogs' eyes,' said Etta, imagining the basket full of them. 'We fry them on Sundays'.

After hogs' eyes Church Lady had fallen quiet, she got off at Albuquerque and Etta slept until Phoenix.

She felt more worn out than she had after all that crying and singing at the funeral. She'd never hear those stories again, never feel those cool hands on her forehead, never see the sun rise over the corn or walk through the rooms of that little wooden house.

When Etta arrived at Union Station there was no one to meet her. She walked across the tiled hall, past rows of candy stands and newspaper stalls, towards an aisle of oak-panelled telephone booths. She entered one and put a dime in the slot.

'That you, Etta?' She heard her father's creaky voice over the line and felt tears burn at the rim of her eyes. She was back now, it had been a long ride.

'Everything's fine,' she said. 'I'll be home in an hour.'

Outside the station, palm trees flapped in the breeze. Across the street, and through a haze of smog-brown air, she could make out the faint line of the San Gabriel Mountains, with the tallest, Mount Baldy, tipped in snow. A few shoe-shine boys were polishing up pairs of office-black shoes. Men in grey pants sat with their legs stretched out on the high pedestal chairs. The boy-men called as she passed.

'Hey Mamma, where you been?'

'Home,' she said, meaning Georgia—even though she hadn't lived there in years. She laughed as one of the boys spat onto a shoe and polished until the leather shone like a pool of oil.

She crossed the wide avenue with its old metal tracks, holding her basket in one hand and the small worn suitcase in the other. A line of yellow taxis stood waiting for passengers as they straggled out of the station. The air was warm and smelled of orange blossom. Turning left, she walked towards the bus on Alameda—tomorrow she'd be back at work at the Langhams'.

Karen Harvey

Flying

As always
restless on terra firma
she longed to take flight
to bathe in the warmth of the sun

So for now she must climb

Allowing the thermals to take her
she continues upwards
up to where the air is thin
the heat unbearable

Too late
meltdown.

Wings singed
she feel herself
plummeting
earthwards.

Migration

At first it was just a prickling under the skin
an itch of scapulae, a lightness in her step
and a longing for blue.

Then she developed an avid interest in
weather forecasts, noting wind speeds,
thermals and felt an urge to sit in high places,
sleeping on the top floor of hotels,
a trip to the Eiffel tower.

At first she was satisfied
but as winter approach
she started sleeping facing South

One morning when she opened
her bedroom window,
it was all too much for her.
A billow of voile
and she was off.

Jo Hemmant

The umpteenth cycle

Flat on my back,
legs splayed in the air
in an athletic V,
hands under my arse
angling my hips, I subject
your slippery deposit
to gravity.

The frontrunner's
half swimming, half falling
down my inhospitable canal,
through the narrow window
in my cervix
into the spongy tissue
of my womb.

There he's on his own—
must thread himself
through the eye
of my kinked left tube,
find the ripe egg
which won't flinch
as he noses exhausted
through its coddled shell.

You're on the far side of the bed,
mute, still—a spent cartridge;
a smoking gun.

The doctor says relax

so we take a holiday in France
where you make me an accidental gift:
the lifecycle of the cicada—
how the female scrapes slits in bark,
lays clutches of eggs like caviar
from which nymphs hatch,
burrow deep
            underground—
a doped colony
suckling on tree roots
for up to seventeen years.

In the final instar,
they bubble up like ground oil,
moult, emerge singing,
ready to mate.

Symptomatic

The first thing I notice
is the sharp smell of must
but can find no trace of mould
on the pristine magnolia walls.

The patch will appear later—
for now the hyphae are dividing,
multiplying in moist cavities
in the brick and plaster;
a growing network of filaments
this side of a broken gutter,
dispersing spores like a lung.

Later the wallpaper will paunch
with the weight of water,
the tidemark creep.

Ian McEwen

The gale blows itself out

because nothing.

Accidental.
One random gust

slams a bird
to the window:
blood on the sheet

and alone.
The bare instinct
'Mummy's OK'. Our son

hands you the phone
blood flows and flown:
nothing because.

That night
you're tired, you're tired
but I can take you

home,
because It's blood you make up
in a week,

because it's a check-up
to bear, one day off,
one 'we'll be OK'

and the solid,
two-year-old
son and I'm

on the phone
if you need, never
alone because home

because accident
one bird because
lost or flown.

Nothing because.
And son grown
and the blood gone

solid, handed on,
long made-up though
so old, new enough.

Random,
the accident
that catches substance,

smear on the sheet
the smear on the glass
still between us. Out there

a bird in the hedge,
              indistinct
final migrant,

last one left
bare on the branch,
                shown

as the random leaves
tear and are gone.
Accident.

Son grown,
and home
somehow small, somehow blown.

I watch as you sleep,
solid, alone,
the blood in your cheek

the hot sheets random.
As you sleep the wind's accidents
      bluster and gust

hand us through hugeness:
      because nothing.
One bird in the gale.

Watch the birdie
Cousins at the seaside, spring 1914

What the birdie
ever was we'll never know.
They're watching it still

though, dressed up
far too tweedy for the beach
and all with hats.

Look how they make
some sense of it, as it (the birdie)
makes its sense of them.

Four chaps (they would
have said) out for a stroll
and turned immortals

on a whim. Caught
by this birdie. They look out past
each fresh moustache

slap-stick into
our comedy
vanishing
point.

Handsfree

The city has no more to say, some nights.
No belly-laughs from busses as they pull
off from the stop, no beads that rattle
over psalms that rise from distant building sites,
no squawks and beeps from tills the barcodes goose.
The churches are all locked up on their blocks
of waxy prayer. No splutterings and plops
come from the coffee stalls, even the tubes
have given over sharpening their paths
and briefly planes accept the sky's been ground
flat enough for now.
                        Then it should come through
handsfree, the conversation's other half:
a double-listening for any sound
of what these are the answer to.

Outpouring

One thing I never knew before was how
—more where— my great-grandmother died: a flat
above a shop in the High Street of this town
I've lived in thirty years since leaving home.
My father never mentioned this before.

It was the early-war when an invasion
panic spread along the coast, aircraft
all sent north of the Humber—they decamped
from—where was it? Teignmouth? The three
of them, my grandmother, great-grandmother,

dad: seven years old as I puzzle it out.
He doesn't have to think. The story flows
from him like time has turned to water
that pours and pours: how these three,
his grandma already sick, limited

by billeting and bombs, could only get
one place. An uncle owned it, three floors up
under the Victorian brow of Bank
Chambers, no place to die, but then where is?
And dad is telling me as if he was

a fountain filling and filling a public
trough, even at night, even if no one
is listening, about her funeral
at what became the Polish Catholic Church,
mock-Saxon effort I pass every day

marooned inside its roundabout, but she,
great-grandma, is buried somewhere else,
on an estate near Haslemere—the old
man who'd been another uncle and MP
and 'loaded' and then that uncle or my

great-grandfather dying in some story
of two ducks—one each barrel—clean shot
that kicked the heart out of him, so he went
happy, or lucky. What is the point of all
that? Why can't I remember it better?

Contributors

David Batten has taught poetry at Coleg Meirion Dwyfor, won the inaugural *Roundyhouse* poetry competition and been twice short-listed for the Cinnamon Press Poetry Collection Award. His fifteen minutes of poetic fame include being asked by Carol Ann Duffy to read a poem at her reading in Machynlleth and helping to put Matthew Sweeney to bed at Llanystumdwy. He lives in France.

Kaddy Benyon worked as a television scriptwriter prior to having children. She started writing poetry in 2009 and her poems have appeared in Spilt Milk, Mslexia, London Magazine, Popshot and are forthcoming in The Frogmore Papers and Stand. She was shortlisted for both the 2010 Fish Poetry Prize and the inaugural Picador Poetry Prize.

Joanna Campbell writes short stories all day at home in the Cotswolds, with three cats and occasional bowls of cereal for company. She has been published in various magazines and anthologies. In 2010, she was shortlisted for the Fish, Bristol and Bridport Short Story Prizes.

Lezanne Clannachan is thirty-seven years old, was born in Denmark and has lived in Brazil, Poland and Singapore. She is currently in West Sussex with her husband and three young children where she runs a local writing group. She is completing her first novel *The Cuckoo-Clock Bride*.

Chris Considine lived for many years in North Yorkshire, before moving to Plymouth in 2011. Her publications include *St. Cuthbert and Bystanders* (Redbeck Press, 2001) and *Swaledale Sketchbook* (Smith/Doorstop Books, 2002). Her first full collection, *Learning to Look*, was published by Peterloo Poets in 2003, followed by *Quarll*, from Peterloo, in 2006. *Behind the Lines* was published by Cinnamon Press in 2011.

Clare Dyer writes women's fiction and works part-time for a London-based HR research forum as well as writing poetry. She was commended in the 2010 Ware Open Poetry Competition and won the 2010 WomenWords poetry competition. She has had poems published by *Orbis, Ragged Raven Press, Envoi* and Leaf Books.

David Ford was born in Devon and lives in East London. His work has been widely published in magazines and a pamphlet collection was published by the HappenStance Press in 2010

Maria Grech Ganado was Born in 1943, a bilingual writer, translator and critic, educated at the Universities of Malta, Cambridge and Heidelberg. She has taught at the University of Malta and other colleges and been invited to international literary events. Her publications include English and Maltese books of poetry and numerous originals and translations in anthologies and journals. She has three children and two grandsons.

Rosie Garland has an eclectic writing and performance history, from 80s Goth band *The March Violets*, to twisted cabaret as alter ego *Rosie Lugosi the Vampire Queen*. With widely anthologised poetry, short stories and essays, she's also won the DaDa Award for Performance Artist of the Year and the Diva Award for Solo Performer.

Gemma Green gained an MA in Creative Writing at UEA with Andrew Motion. In 2008 she won 2nd prize in the *Daily Telegraph* Poetry for Performance competition and this year won 2nd prize in the Plough International Poetry Competition. In 2010 Gemma was selected by the Arvon Foundation for their Jerwood Mentoring scheme and spent a year being mentored by Jo Shapcott.

Gabriel Griffin is the founder (2001) and organiser of Poetry on the Lake competition and events on Lake Orta, Italy, ; editor of annual anthologies and Journal. Prized and placed in numerous competitions, published in Temenos, Scintilla, Peterloo, HQ, Poetry.

Karen Harvey lives in the coastal town of Pwllheli. She facilitates creative writing workshops in the community and her poems, articles and short stories have been published in anthologies, magazines and on-line. She is currently working toward her first poetry collection with a mentor provided by Literature Wales.

Jacqueline Haskell began writing drama in her teens and she turned down a place at Oxford for a career in the theatre. She has an MA in Creative Writing from Birkbeck, University of London, and her stories have been shortlisted for both the Fish Short Story Prize and the Asham Award. She is currently working on her first novel, *The Auspice*.

Vivian Hassan-Lambert's work has appeared in BBC Brazen Radio, Half-Empty Bookcase, Jewish Chronicle, Lillian Baylis Theatre, Momaya Review, PulpNet, QWF and TellTales 4 Anthology. She was short-listed for the Bridport 2010 and Serpents Tail London Short Story awards and is a recipient of an Arts Council Grant for the Arts. She lives in London with her husband and daughter. *Jericho* grew from a section of her forthcoming novel set in 1960s Los Angeles.

Jo Hemmant lives with her family in rural Kent. Her poems have appeared in various magazines and anthologies and she has won prizes in competitions. Last year she decided to combine her many years of experience in publishing with her love of poetry and set up Pindrop Press.

Lindsey Holland's poetry and reviews have appeared in publications including *Tears in the Fence, Ink, Sweat & Tears* and *The Oxfam Anthology of Young British Poets*. Her pamphlet *Particle Soup* will be published this year. She is Poetry Editor for *Sabotage Reviews* and is the founder member of North West Poets. She blogs at http://particlesoup.blogspot.com.

Anthony Howcroft is a writer and technology entrepreneur whose stories have appeared in many journals and anthologies. He's the founder of Ink Tears, a site championing the cause of the short story. Anthony has a Creative Writing Diploma from Oxford University and two Weimaraner dogs that bark during important phone calls.

Rosalind Hudis, from Tregaron, is studying for an MA in Creative Writing at TSD Lampeter. She won the 2011 Wilfred Owen Bursary. She has had work published by several respected journals and was a runner up in Cinnamon Press's Snow and Ice in Verse competition. One of her poems won a commendation in the 2011 National Poetry Competition.

Anna Johnson is a founder member of the Forest Poets collective based in North London. She has had work in five anthologies of new British writing including Lung Jazz: the Oxfam Book of Young British Poets (Cinnamon Press, 2012).

Alex Josephy lives in the East End of London and works in the NHS as an education adviser. She has had poems published in *The Rialto, Smiths Knoll, The Interpreter's House* and others. In 2010 she won a second prize in the Hippocrates competition, and was placed in the Troubadour top twenty.

Phil Madden lives in Wales. He travels Europe as a Disability Consultant .His work has appeared in many anthologies and magazines. He has written two limited edition books "Wings Take Us" and" 39 Faces of the Urban Moon" with renowned engravers Paul Kershaw and Peter Lazarov.

Ian McEwen studied philosophy and then worked in investment banking before returning to writing in 2002. His poems have appeared in *Smiths Knoll*, *Poetry Wales* and *Poetry Review* among others. He is on the board of *Magma*. His pamphlet *The Stammering Man* was a winner in the Templar competition 2010. His collection *Father lost lost* is forthcoming from Cinnamon Press.

Melanie Whipman

MWS

Jane McLaughlin writes poetry and short stories. *A Roof of Red Tiles* is the title story of this anthology. Her work has appeared in several other Cinnamon Press publications and in a wide range of magazines and anthologies. She wrote a series of poems about the Titanic disaster after visiting Halifax, Nova Scotia in 2010; two of them are published here.

Eithne Nightingale works as Head of Diversity and Equality at the V&A Museum and has published extensively on the arts and diversity. She has also had publications of travel, fiction and memoir writing in the UK and Australia and has won or been runner up in writing competitions. She is a keen photographer. For more of her work visit: www.eithnenightingale.com.

David Olsen second poetry chapbook, *New World Elegies*, is new from Finishing Line Press. His work has been published in dozens of British and American journals; since 2008 his poems have appeared in *Envoi*, *Acumen*, *Orbis*, *Assent*, *The Interpreter's House*, *Poetry Nottingham*, *Oxford Magazine*, *Writing Magazine* and competition anthologies.

Edward Ragg was born in Stockton-on-Tees and lives in Beijing. His first volume of poetry, *A Force That Takes*, is forthcoming from Cinnamon. His poems have appeared in numerous magazines and anthologies including New Poetries IV (Carcanet, 2007). He is an Associate Professor at Tsinghua University and co-founder of Dragon Phoenix Wine Consulting.

Marcus Smith's work has appeared in *Ambit, Acumen, PN Review, Prairie Schooner, Salzburg Poetry Review* and *The South Carolina Review*.

Lindsey Stanberry-Flynn taught English in further and higher education before giving up to concentrate on writing. She has an MA in creative writing from Bath Spa University. Her first novel, *Unravelling*, was published in June 2010, and her novel, *The Piano Player's Son*, is forthcoming from Cinnamon Press. Her short stories have been successful in competitions such as The Fish International Short Story Prize and the Asham Award for Women Writers. Lindsay lives in Worcestershire where she teaches creative writing.

Jill Teague is a poet and Certified Poetry Therapist based in Snowdonia, North Wales. Much of her writing is inspired by the natural world. She is a writing tutor and Assistant Director of The International Academy for Poetry Therapy, NYC. She leads writing workshops in Wales and the USA.

Aisling Tempany has appeared in four previous Cinnamon Press anthologies since 2009, as well as recently appearing in the Templar Press anthology *Bliss*. She lives in Wales, and is studying part-time as a postgraduate in Swansea University, writing on Irish Modernists.

Frances Corkey Thompson reads her work regularly at Arts Centres and Festivals. She has a Poetry MA with distinction from Exeter University. Her work appears in many magazines and anthologies. Her chapbook, *The Long Acre*, was published by Happenstance in 2008.

Nicola Warwick lives in Suffolk where she works in local government. She has had poems in various magazines, as well as prizes in competitions. She has twice been a finalist in the Cinnamon Press Poetry Collection Award.

Noel Williams is widely published in anthologies and magazines, including *Iota, Envoi, The North* and *Wasafiri*, and has won fifty prizes and commendations. He was Resident Poet at Sheffield's Bank Street Arts Centre, with a highly successful exhibition, Exploding Poetry. He's a lecturer and a student at Sheffield Hallam University, and runs writing workshops for local organisations.

Richard Williams

Martin Willitts Jr poems appear in *Storm at Galesburg and other stories* (international anthology). His tenth chapbook is *The Garden of French Horns* (Pudding House Publications, 2008) and his second full length book of poetry is *The Hummingbird* (March Street Press, 2009. He is co-editor of Hot Metal Press.

Margaret Wilmot studied at the University of California in Berkeley before taking jobs in Italy and Greece. She has lived in Sussex since 1978. Sources of interest and inspiration keep expanding and changing but at present include the connections based on memory, natural history, painting, science, life.

Patricia Helen Wooldridge lives in Hampshire and is inspired by landscape and nature. She has a doctorate in creative writing and until recently taught creative writing to undergraduate students. Her poetry has been published in a variety of poetry magazines including *The London Magazine, Interpreter's House, Iota, and Staple*.